Approximation Zero

A Philosophical Framework for Artificial General Intelligence

By Mike Archbold

Contact: jazzbox35@gmail.com

Published in the United States of America by Michael P Archbold

Cover Photography by Mike Archbold

First Edition

ISBN – 13   978-0-615-88281-9

Special thanks to Peter Voss and Penguin Books for permission to quote from works and to Laura Kerns for the author photograph.

Contents

Chapter 1: Why AI?

Introduction

What is the motivation for AI that would yield human-level intelligence? The short answer is so that you don't have to drag yourself out of bed to go to work – some machine could do your job in place of you.   But let us take a somewhat closer look at this topic in this chapter.

No one presently has been known to have developed human-level artificial intelligence. Within the course of about the last ten years a relatively small group within and on the fringes of the AI community has tried to alter the course of AI away from heavily constrained applications toward applications applicable in a completely general manner, a human-level manner. Ben Goertzel is a chief proponent of this influential movement and widely credited with popularizing the phrase "artificial general intelligence," abbreviated AGI, standing in contrast to the traditional AI abbreviation. Note that "general" is inserted to signal the drive toward general, not specific, application functionality.

The book *Artificial General Intelligence* describes some of the many efforts underway in AGI. Peter Voss, founder of Adaptive AI, writes that "*General* intelligence comprises the *essential, domain-independent skills* necessary for acquiring a wide range of domain-specific knowledge (data and skills) – i.e., the ability to learn anything (in principle). More specifically, this learning ability needs to be autonomous, goal-directed, and highly adaptive..."[1]

The key phrase is "domain-independent," because at this stage virtually all technology is intended for some fairly narrowly defined purpose within a well-known domain. Yet what we ultimately need is the equivalent of a program that can literally do *everything*. This book tries to

establish a philosophical framework as a potential
starting point for that goal. Were such a mechanism built
to automate this level of intelligence the scope of
applications would obviously be staggering.

But for the moment, regardless of what we call AI, be it
human-level, strong or weak AI, AGI, narrow, general, or
what have you, the sober fact is that more than 50 years
of experience has shown simply that no single solution is
yet able to handle the actual complexities needed for
actual artificial intelligence, of the sort that truly
seems human-level. What is more, if we grant Aristotle
the honor of being the first AI researcher – having
invented term logic this is arguably justified – we are
obliged to add more than 2000 years to this effort. The
Dartmouth conference in 1956, however, is generally
regarded as the kickoff of AI. This conference on AI
ambitiously stated[source wikipedia]:

"We propose that a 2 month, 10 man study of artificial
intelligence be carried out during the summer of 1956 at
Dartmouth College in Hanover, New Hampshire. The study is
to proceed on the basis of the conjecture that every
aspect of learning or any other feature of intelligence
can in principle be so precisely described that a machine
can be made to simulate it. An attempt will be made to
find how to make machines use language, form abstractions
and concepts, solve kinds of problems now reserved for
humans, and improve themselves. We think that a
significant advance can be made in one or more of these
problems if a carefully selected group of scientists work
on it together for a summer."

Well, a single summer did not allocate enough time. Fifty
plus years of experience has shown primarily that humans
seem to be good at abstracting elements of thinking and
behavior into our programmed devices, but most
emphatically not at unifying all aspects of experience in
these devices. The bottom line is that if we program in
carefully constrained abstractions we are successful, but
approaches that aim to solve a panorama of arbitrarily
complex real-world problems without recourse to specific
preprogramming are out of reach.

But let us not forget that artificial intelligence has
been successful – albeit in a form derisively known in
the 21st century, and especially by advocates of AGI, as
"narrow AI," but more positively as "practical AI."
Chiefly this approach features the automation of

essentially an extreme autistic savant unable to solve
problems beyond its particular heavily constrained domain
– as for example the noteworthy expert system *Deep Blue*,
IBM's grand master equivalent chess program. More recent
efforts are more impressive, such as IBM's *Watson*. Still,
Watson seems to follow a fairly well structured
interaction format, making it difficult to determine how
well it will perform in other more varied problem
situations.

General intelligence, it should seem clear, seems to be
based upon certain basic principles applied consistently,
uniformly, and ubiquitously that if correctly defined and
implemented should result in the solution to arbitrary
problems – not just problems which are highly defined and
constrained. A solution to the general intelligence
problem tantalizingly seems within the limits of our
capabilities – it seems more so all the time – in spite
of so many difficulties, dead ends, and downright setbacks
experienced by researchers and practitioners down through
the years.

Not accepting defeat Goertzel and others stubbornly carry
on the quest, outlined in the original Dartmouth
conference, towards true, general artificial intelligence.
The stakes are high. A solution to a broad class of
general arbitrary problems with a full-blown general
artificial intelligence opens huge vistas. To the extent
that automated general intelligence is successful we will
experience significant social improvements. Three are
described here.

Total Cost Eliminations and Virtually Unlimited Potential Functionalities

Total cost eliminations and virtually unlimited potential
functionalities are conceivable by automating and
expanding upon virtually all present forms of human
endeavor. This can be visualized as a continuum ranging
from simple, repetitive manual labor tasks to the
application of virtually any sort of expertise. The
maximum possible availability of any sort of help to do
anything possible at the lowest possible cost is actually
conceivable.

Some functions simply cannot be performed by a human being at all, such as tasks involving incredibly high speed and precision. Robots can venture into dangerous territory.

We can envision the same sort of cognitive processing engine used generally as a basis in all manner of general applications, whether traditional computational processing or embodied robotics.

The Elimination of the Expert

To a great extent human society is stratified socially and economically based upon occupation. Physician is the most socially prestigious occupation and street sweeper the least. Airline pilot and architect are more prestigious occupations than either electrician or jazz musician.[2]

It seems impossible to separate the person from the occupation and in fact there simply is a positive incentive to join a person to his occupation and judge him accordingly. In an earlier age, a carpenter may well change his name to Carpenter, a smith to Smith and so forth. In the modern age, persons obtaining doctorates still change their names and frequently carry this appellation to the grave. It is not uncommon to see "M.D." appearing on a tombstone, as an example.   I have also seen "Judge" appearing on a tombstone. No one writes "street sweeper" on their tombstone - or so one suspects.

Anecdotally I have known someone who made a point of associating with physicians, even though her occupation had nothing to do with health care and in the course of her daily affairs she would otherwise not associate with physicians except in a patient context. No such effort however was observed in a corresponding fashion to befriend persons of more common and lesser social stature. The strong presumption obviously is that she sought to advance herself socially.

We seem to be segregated as a society based largely (although certainly not exclusively) upon each individual person's accumulation of some "stock of knowledge = X." This stock-of-knowledge = X would in general terms include rules of application, methods, proficiencies, certifications, standards of behavior whether clearly documented or as some obscure black art, unwritten rules for personal airs as appropriate, and invariably always some seemingly ancient, tiresome, secret insider lexicon – such as legalese and health care terminology. These practices seem devised in part to be incomprehensible to the layperson, thus helping to make a very clear distinction between the profession in question and persons outside the profession.

Can we envision a society that puts an end to the constant social connection between a person and occupation, or simply put can we put an end to the connection between any person and his stock-of-knowledge = X? Can we put an end experts? Can we put an end to the phrase "I am a..." something? Can we see social stratification based upon occupation as mere temporary evolutionary development of the human race which as a side effect includes a long practiced social and occupational bias? Possibly we can view occupational bias in the same negative way that we view racial and sexist prejudice.

If AI were to take over occupational roles, no longer will we need to "be" a "something," such as surveyor or geologist or anything ending in "-er," "-ist," and "-or." It would no longer be Dr. Smith M.D. but just Mr. Smith who is no better or worse than anyone else based upon his occupation = X and stock-of-knowledge = X. We will no longer have to say "John is a..." and John will no longer have to act like everybody else in his profession. Jane will not seek out the company of John simply because of his stock-of-knowledge = X and his association with others holding the stock-of-knowledge = X. He will no longer have to wear similar clothing and adopt similar speech patterns and predictable modes of behavior to fit in with his colleagues and their stock-of-knowledge = X.

Indeed there would be no colleagues. You wouldn't have to drag yourself out of bed every morning and work with people you may dislike under possibly unhealthy circumstances. Life would be one long weekend.

A Counterbalance to Human Reasoning

Nietzsche wrote the following which I take to be a reasonable description of human behavior: "...how wretched, how shadowy and flighty, how aimless and arbitrary, the human intellect appears in nature. There

have been eternities when it did not exist; and when it is
done for again, nothing will have happened."[3]

Human beings are often biased, lazy, manic, prone to
addictions, heavily pressured socially, inconsistent,
emotional, quarrelsome, prone to health problems,
obsessive, irresponsible, daydreamers, tribal, nepotistic,
too readily willing to proceed upon the default
assumptions, prejudiced, forgetful, and so on. And that
is just on the good days! I have never seen any
compelling reason to hold human reasoning as some sort of
gold standard.

As an example of human bias, consider jury selection. It
is common to start with a group of fifty potential jurors
just to find twelve unbiased enough - or more accurately,
biased correctly - to sit on the panel.

We could use some help. A machine can display perfect
memory, precision, speed, consistency, tirelessness,
obedience, and so forth, and can conceivably be programmed
to behave in an ethical manner.

Yet a computer is simply not a human being. It is a
machine and should not aspire to be humanlike in the sense
outlined above. Some researchers and practitioners would
like to equip machines to act identically to human beings
acting emotionally. Can you imagine your computer acting
like a human being? Acting biased? Too tired to work?
Calling in sick today? Not wishing to follow our
instructions but instead deciding to argue?

A computer should long continue to be a stable, rational,
and logical servant to a human being but with greatly
expanded functionality - importantly maintaining its basic
essence as described above. A computer could still
empathize without itself reacting emotionally. A computer
should not lose its remarkable attributes in an attempt to
be like a human in the misguided pursuit of artificial
intelligence. A human being is not the gold standard of
intelligence.

That bears repeating. It should be no goal to recreate
human reasoning using the sort of intellect that Nietzsche
seems to have fairly realistically described.

Yet, in order to deal with the real diversity of problems normally handled by human experts basic extensions to computers are simply unavoidable. Current architectures and approaches seem simply inadequate to achieve general intelligence that would function in the real world. But that does not mean that the essence of the computer should really change. A computer should always be a reliable and helpful agent.

Consider this famous quote by Hume: "Reason is, and ought only to be the slave of the passions, and can never pretend to any other office than to serve and obey them."[4] If we were to substitute a computer equipped with artificial general intelligence for "reason" and human being for "passions" above we would have an ideal computer-human interaction model to aspire to.

The computer should always be (amongst other things) a very stable goal-seeking ethical servant acting as a counterbalance to unpredictable and frequently misguided human behavior.

Throughout this book, I will use the acronym AI exclusively, although what is meant is "strong AI," the equivalent to AGI, artificial general intelligence, the objective of the original Dartmouth conference. I don't mean narrow, constrained, and heavily preprogrammed AI.

The Bottom Line

In summary, AI could solve seemingly intractable economic, social, and philosophical problems:

> 1) Enabling tremendous cost reductions while increasing potential functionalities – the economic reason.

> 2) Ending social biases based upon occupation – the social reason.

> 3) Functioning as a correcting counterbalance to irrational human behavior – the philosophical reason.

The most problematic features of actual strong AI are arguably the likelihood of simply being saturated in technology and the worthy fear of computers making poor critical decisions beyond our control. We must bear in mind that there is a strong choice factor in the use of technology. Just because a technology is available for a specific problem does not mean we need to use it, and if we do use a technology, it must be done judiciously. We must always accept the responsibilities in the use of technology and exercise prudent choices. A computer must always be under our control. We should only cede as much control as we safely choose to a computer.

Furthermore, the pursuit of AI technology should never be for the sake of love of such technology. The goal of this sort of technology is for the functionality that it provides which will yield the benefits as illustrated above. This issue will become more and more important as we become increasingly saturated in technology.

Again: the critical point is that we must exercise prudent choices over how we use AI (for that matter any technology) for the sake of the good it will do for society.

And then what do we do? Chiefly we can pursue the arts with our friends and engage in the contemplative life, which Aristotle described as the highest form of activity.[5]

Artificial intelligence, given its possible advantages and problems, can be seen primarily as a massive social issue.

Chapter 2: A Philosophical Framework Based Upon Mind and Matter

Introduction

In this chapter, we examine some of the problems surrounding contemporary AI, I point out the need for a philosophical framework, I provide a philosophical framework, then given the nature of this new framework we can begin to see what characteristics a new AI could and should arguably have.

The philosophical framework herein is a hybrid original construct designed as a starting point for AI. I can't take credit for all ideas in the framework. It draws heavily upon ideas developed originally by the well known thinkers listed in the "Works Consulted For the Philosophical Framework" bibliography whose work would be foolish to ignore. The ideas of Hegel, in particular, strongly influence the framework. In general it should be obvious where I have coined my own terms, *but if there is any doubt about the origin of any part of the philosophical matrix credit is to be assigned to one or more of the legendary philosophers listed in the "Works Consulted" bibliography*. Philosophers typically build upon prior works anyway, so we have a bit of a muddle in assigning credit.

Many AI approaches begin with a general definition of intelligence, then present a strategy for implementation usually with some new method(s) built with Turing computation. That is fine if it works, but this strategy is somewhat different.

Here we do not take Turing computation along with a definition of intelligence as a starting point. Instead we are going to look at reality as a whole and try to tease out some of its most glaring and simple features. We will build a classification of reality in a fairly structured way, and then hope we can determine *what* AI could do and *how* based upon the sorts of constraints and regularities we find.

Thinking Seems Different Than the Turing Machine

Alan Turing is rightly regarded as the father of the computer. His Turing machine, an imaginary machine introduced in 1936, is a logical machine.[6] Turing envisioned it to consist of a tape, read/write head, state register, and table (i.e., the program). I will use the phrases "Turing machine" and "Turing computation" as equivalent to the modern, typical computer, since firstly a modern computer can be simulated on a Turing machine and secondly because we seem to easily relate the phrase to any typical computer. There are equivalents, variations, and extensions to the Turing machine but they will not, in general, be discussed here.

Turing computation saturates virtually all areas of contemporary computing including AI. Even though we can with multiple layers of software abstraction resort to varied paradigms, for example neural networks, in general the typical Turing input/output state machine permeates virtually all levels of modern computing. It seems difficult for anyone who has ever written a line of code to think of computing in ways inconsistent with the Turing machine. Yet, alternatives strategies do exist, notably hypercomputation, a relatively young field devoted to pushing the boundaries beyond Turing computing.

The Turing Machine Is Not Well Suited for Metaphysics

The Turing machine seems really quite a bit different from a thinking mind, at first glance seeming like a fancy calculator designed by mathematicians to run as fast and deterministically as possible.

In his initial conception of a computer, Turing envisioned the computer as a person, since in those days a "computer" was indeed a person hired for routine calculations. The computer man executed a given procedure in a "desultory" manner, putting little thought into the matter save what was required for his fixed procedures.

Using that as an initial basis upon which all progress has been made, it should come as no surprise that artificial intelligence has struggled to advance beyond mere desultory computation. That is all that seemed to be really intended at the outset. The computer man was not hired to do any thinking. The computer man's instructions were specified for him.

While the fundamental research that led to the computer was driven by brilliant mathematicians, philosophers, and logicians, there was seemingly no initial attempt to build into the design such commonsense rules of reality such as "something exists but I can't see it" or "something does not physically exist but I can see it," (like a rainbow) or that "something might cause something else," or that "a beginning always precedes the end," or time, or really much of what we associate with the rest of the most basic rules of everyday reality. In general metaphysics was left out.

Rather, the computer seems to have been intended initially more as a fast calculator which presumes or leaves blank bigger metaphysical issues – such issues being essential to what we associate with thinking. The argument was that so long as an algorithm could be formulated, it could be implemented on a Turing machine. But there was never any sort of fundamental ontology basis *from which to build an algorithm upon*, no supporting structure, for example, that represented self which knew it was not the same thing as its algorithm.

I don't think there is any doubt that the standard essence of a computer, descended down from the days of Turing, is fundamentally a mathematical device. Granted logic stems from a philosophical source, which along with mathematics can be closely related, still, there probably never was an initial attempt to build a robust ontology, of the sort we might get from Aristotle, directly into the most fundamental design of the computer. Quickly we saw operators for addition and subtraction, for example, but not operators we might see in Aristotle's metaphysical lexicon like "beginning," "cause," "limit."[7] Down through the years we've had to make awkward attempts at building an ontology on top of the basic Turing machine design, which we generally take to be mathematical in origin, and the fixed, sole, and canonical method of computing.

How can a computer that does not have such basic metaphysical distinctions as "something appears" or "something does not appear" at the most fundamental level, such as the equivalent of the machine instruction level, ever aspire to anything truly like what we associate with thinking?

The Machine Is Programmed Externally by a Person With Ideas

In the Turing machine the processing performed is defined beforehand by a programmer, externally to the machine. It is a programmed machine. The computer has little immanent connectivity within its data apart from physical proximity, no idea what it's doing, being dependent exclusively upon control specified outside of itself.

Searle's legendary "Chinese Room" argument illustrates this problem well.[8] The computer just follows instructions having no idea what it is doing, indeed having no idea what an idea is, and no reference to a self. Such a scenario can hardly be described as thinking. In thinking, for starters, sense impressions appear immediately connected to memory and rational thinking processes, and there is no direct reliance on programmed control from without.

Machine Input and Output (I/O) Seems Different Than the Human Counterparts

One of the most pervasive concepts in all of computing is the notion of input and output. Input to a machine is of course a radically different thing than its output. It would be impossible to even conceive of modern computing without the clear input/output dichotomy. A typical AI chess game inputs the present board configuration, outputs its next move, then waits for the opponent to move before input of the next board configuration.

Yet, in our own thinking experience, obvious upon even a moment's consideration, we find that firstly *everything seems to be constantly input, a* notion that may seem strange at first. Experience presents a single,

integrated, and continuous manifold of "input" which in
general *contains whatever we deem as output*, such as
speech and movement. Speech is immediately registered as
input to the mind. Simple, discrete, abstract input and
output forms the basis of seemingly all modern computing
interactions. It is a perfectly useful abstraction, but
not really the same as the human experience of input and
output. Pervasive, universal, and continuous closed loop
feedback seems a much more accurate depiction of thinking
than a simple input/output dichotomy.

Thinking provides a single input totality from which we
can make distinctions. Yet, the sort of distinctions that
thinking makes have much more to do with cause and effect
operating within a single input manifold than with input
and output as independent concepts. Again, speech is
registered immediately as input to the mind at the same
instant that it is caused – output – by the person
speaking. More will be said about input and output below.
But for the moment, note that one of the most fundamental
metaphysical issues, such as cause and effect, essential
for thinking, was initially ignored in light of the more
pressing need to make a calculating machine, the computer,
which was conceived as a rigid input and output device.

The Computer Often Ignores Wall Clock Time

Anyone who has ever programmed a computer knows that the
issue of time comes immediately into play: in general, we
simply want the program to run as fast as possible. At a
given time the computer is in a specific state. At the
next processing cycle in sequence the machine is in the
same or different state, or the program has halted. The
general goal has always been that the computer runs as
fast as possible while making sure that at any given time
it is in the correct state. Fast execution speed is
generally of the utmost importance. Nobody wants to wait
for their computer. Occasionally the computer must wait
for input, say from a user, or wait for an unavailable
resource, but if it is not waiting we want it to run as
fast as possible.

But the problem with this conception is that it evidently
ignores or makes secondary commonsense wall clock time,
upon which ordinary experience is seemingly entirely
based. Evolution did not craft our minds to run
particularly fast, at least relative to a modern computer.
Since the goal of evolution does not seem to have been to
craft a mind simply to work as fast as possible (although

plainly we can at some times think faster than at other times), we are justified in asking the question: why then is the mind so slow relative to a computer? Could it be that there is some necessary synchronization needed between the speed with which our minds work relative to the progression of everyday physical events?

It does seems that thoughts do progress roughly in harmony with the timing of everyday, worldly, analog events. If I happen to pour myself a cup of coffee, the coffee does not pour out of the carafe as fast as conceivably possible! Granted that this is an unscientific point, but it does seem to me that my mind works at a relatively slow sort of speed that is easily synchronized with everyday events.

The Computer Has Distinct States but Humans Have Mixed and Muddled States

The Turing machine is a state machine. We can easily examine what state the machine is in at any point in execution by pausing its operation and looking at the contents of its state register. The state register can contain one state value drawn from the finite set of states defined for the machine. This sounds simple enough. What Turing apparently had in mind for "state" was like a person's state of mind *as it specifically relates to the specific circumstances of the computation presently in progress.*

It is not so easy to actually determine the state of a person, although clearly Turing had this analogy in mind. Is a thinking person a state machine? At any given instant can we define a specific personal state? To some extent it seems so, but usually when we refer to the state a person is in, we mean an emotional state, or possibly present activity state, or some expected probable future state, or some state due to past state, or any sort of such a combination.

John is happy. Jane is contemplating a movie. Ralph is happily contemplating a movie. We can keep adding qualifying clauses to the present state. We can start adding clauses that concern transition, such as John's state is that he is happy because he has just left a bad movie and is joining Jane who is contemplating a different movie she heard about from Ralph who likes it because it relates to a certain life experience he had while living in an orphanage. Take that for our present state. For general problems, combinatorial explosion is likely to quickly emerge making the total number of states unwieldy and infinite.

Turing's states seems to only work well for carefully constrained problems of the sort amenable to narrow AI solutions. What seems to be missing in Turing computation is something equivalent to our mysterious ability which enables us to convert and represent complicated situations with a great many potential states and nuances *into a single, continuous yet changing understood idea*. Such ideas seem to change smoothly essentially in harmony with commonsense wall-clock time and developing events.

Summary

In summary, given these considerations we see that thinking seems to be significantly different than the canonical Turing state machine, upon which virtually all of modern computing including artificial intelligence is based.

Thinking Seems Different Than Material Things in General

This is a perennial philosophical mind-body problem. Is mind the same sort of thing as matter which occupies space? How does mind communicate with body and the rest of physical matter?

Descartes and Dualism

Philosophy has long debated this issue but it was really Descartes that kicked off the modern formulations of the problem. On one end of the spectrum Descartes claimed that the mind is completely separate from the realm of physical, spatial extension. He theorized that communication between mind and body, two different substances, was made possible by the convenient intermediary pineal gland (which was basically simply a wild guess not taken very seriously even in his day). Spinoza thought that mind and body were the same thing, the same substance, an absolute God, but merely different

20

attributes of God operating in unison. Other approaches such as Berkeley's claimed that there simply was no realm of extension at all – a convenience which sort of nullified the whole argument – since ideas are all that we experience, then ideas are all that exist.

In the present age it is not fashionable nor really acceptable at all to hold to these sorts of philosophies nor their variations, at least anywhere beyond the walls of a university philosophy department or your local spiritual bookstore. This sort of discussion is not deemed a particularly good use of time to most engineers that design AI. I doubt the topic is brought up much by our typical rock star engineer. Engineers are taught to design machines using well known physical sciences drawn exclusively from what Descartes would call the spatial extension part of reality. There seems to exist a pervasive climate of opinion, as in the doctrine of physicalism, that all aspects of the universe can presently or eventually be accounted for strictly in terms of physical and material causes. Of course this would include the phenomena of mind, that mind is not something radically different nor separate from physical matter.

That may be. But, it does seem obvious, though, that regardless of which viewpoint one holds, be it a physics-centric, idea-centric, some compromise like dualism, or a personal viewpoint dependent upon how much time you prefer to spend around physics or philosophy, that *the thought of car keys is simply not the same thing as car keys*. You don't have to be a philosopher to pick up on the idea that those are two different things, regardless of how you account for the universe. Call this the "car keys test."

As another example to illustrate the difference between the physical and the mental consider the concept "boundary." The usage of the word to describe some physical formation that we may see such as the Great Wall of China has a similar meaning to its usage with respect to the contents of everyday thinking, such as whatever it is that mentally separates distinct episodes in my life. The basic idea holds true for both mind and matter, that of separation of distinct things, but the meaning is somewhat different. A mental boundary is just not the same thing as a wall's boundary, but it is not altogether different either.

Suppose we suddenly hit upon the idea that we could use a system of several physical walls to model episodic

memories. After all, we might be thinking initially, a
physical boundary is the same as a mental one, so it will
work! Suppose we decided to place within each compartment
divided by walls some representation of each memory, say a
photograph of each episode to be modeled. Everything is
fine so far. But now suppose we want to add to our memory
model the ability to find similarities between the
memories, or account for which order they happened in, or
devise a means of remembering the episodes based upon
relevance to some activity, such as driving, or ranking by
cost, or adding the cost of each episode and dividing by
the total to find the average cost of each episode.

It should be starting to look like a physical boundary
such as a wall is not quite the same thing as a mental
boundary such as the that which divides distinct thoughts.
I can somehow think of two related episodes at once. I
can think of playing in two separate football games in
separate places at once in a single combined thought that
compares games. But I cannot be physically standing on
two separate football fields at once. The mental boundary
that divides memories of two games can easily be bridged,
but not so with a physical boundary.

Now suppose that I wanted to create a mental model of the
Great Wall of China. I cannot construct a physical little
Great Wall of China in my head. That rules out
immediately the prospect of a material, physical boundary
inside my head. You get the idea.

The point is that it should be plainly obvious that mind
and matter are not the same. There is a difference. How
these types of things are different – a thought vs. a
physical object – seems to be a *very important question in
the context of AI*. It has long been an important issue in
philosophy, and contemporary writers such as Chalmers,[9]
Dennett,[10] and Penrose[11] have differing views on the roles
of consciousness and physics.

Part of the problem with AI is the profoundly questionable
notion that mental operations can be duplicated simply
using tools found in the physical world, such as
transistors and logic gates, without adequately taking
into consideration the similarities and differences
between the physical and mental realms. The two are
similar, but seem not entirely the same. This situation
is not always simply taken for granted however: Intel and
IBM have both been working on chips designed to work
physically more like a human brain.

It's very important to *not* gloss over this problem because
the method of AI is traditionally consistent with the
Turing machine which, in the form of a standard computer,
follows the laws of physics as we see in the realm of
matter.   But if mind is *at the very least* different than
physical, spatial reality, as we see in the simple car
keys test, then in what ways is it different? In what
ways is it the same?

A Philosophical Framework Should Be Part of Any AI Approach

Now having stated some of the difficulties which confront
us above, it seems clear that there is a great deal of
uncertainty regarding the basic grounds of artificial
intelligence. Firstly, the contemporary computer seems to
operate much differently than a mind. Secondly, there
exists longstanding contention regarding the relation of
mind to the rest of physical reality. That might not be
such a big problem except that we are trying to model the
mind with tools we find in physical reality! We have not
even defined what intelligence *is* and debate surrounds
this topic. Psychology provides definitions for more than
one type of intelligence.

Avoiding this muddle to some extent, most AI (and as a
reminder when I say AI I mean "strong AI" or "artificial
general intelligence") approaches seem to skirt around
these perennial difficulties and pragmatically approach
the problem by stating generally what intelligence is in
their model, how a proposed novel design usually built
using Turing computation will create such an intelligence,
and then proceeding to implement.

Of course, if these approaches work there is nothing wrong
with delaying or bypassing addressing those perennially
difficult issues as stated above, and much time may be
saved. After all, heavy issues in philosophy and
psychology have long been contentious and defy
straightforward definition. Issues in metaphysics are
also simply burdened by a negative connotation. Mario
Bunge's *Philosophical Dictionary* defines metaphysics in
the "common sense" usage as "pompous nonsense..."[12] The
challenge may well be if "pompous nonsense" can ever be

tempered and refined enough to serve as a starting
platform for strong AI.

We Won't Start With a Definition of Intelligence And Turing Computation

But let's suppose that instead of taking the usual route –
defining basically what intelligence is and how a novel
design built with Turing computation would work – we
instead gamely created an initial "philosophical
framework" which models as best we can some of the issues
described above, such as the nature of mind versus matter,
how they are similar, related, differ, and interact. The
framework would also hopefully make plain how we could
accommodate AI with respect to the mind-body problem.

Reality – of which mind is plainly a part – appears to be
presenting us with all manner of constraints,
regularities, categories, types, rules, and other such
issues that make up its system. In constructing a
philosophical framework we force ourselves to look at the
big picture first so that hopefully the nature of
intelligence can be more readily ascertained, not by using
our own definition of intelligence in conjunction with a
Turing machine, but rather by looking at *essentially all
of reality* and seeing what intelligence is and how it fits
into the big picture. Ignoring the mind-body problem,
planning to devise clever algorithms, and then placing all
our faith in the Church-Turing thesis seems to only go so
far. We can always dispense with our preconceptions of AI
in the same sort of spirit that Descartes dispensed with
all beliefs he could somehow doubt. We can try to take a
fresh look at what reality is telling us about itself.

It is well worth noting that the answers to these
questions necessary for the philosophical framework have
as their motivation some form of AI tractability and not
necessarily absolute truth. There has never been a
philosophical system that has been shown to be beyond
criticism. Philosophy is the source of endless
argumentation. It *is* the art and science of
argumentation. A philosophical system developed in the
pursuit of artificial intelligence will show its truth
simply in its perceived effectiveness – and let us
realize that the more effective some philosophic system
implemented actually is, the more true a representation of
reality it will appear to have.

24

Why not start with a more mathematically-oriented framework instead of a philosophical framework? Starting basically with the Pythagoreans there has probably always been a class of persons that think that mathematics can account for virtually everything in reality. A very large portion of AI research is predicated firmly upon mathematical techniques.

But what are grounds for the reliance upon mathematics in AI? What is presented to our minds as we think is a single, integrated, immaterial totality within which we can possess certain fairly discrete ideas. Mathematics seems to have been based initially upon discrete mental abstractions – in other words, basically ideas – required to quantify physical and material external occurrences. For example, an idea of the count of warriors in an enemy tribe may well have been the sort of thought our ancestors had.

If we are aiming for a human-level AI, that means we need our AI to have something like ideas. It is not clear at all how formalizing a set of mathematical ideas leads directly to the formation or automation of the *idea itself* as we require in AI. In the first place a mathematical idea is *already an idea.* It is ideas of a general nature, including but also beyond quantifying ideas, that we seek.

Summary

In summary, the goal of starting development using a base philosophical framework is an overall definition of how the AI fits into reality by exposing constraints, properties, and requirements that might otherwise be obscured. To the extent that an implemented philosophical system appears to work it can be considered "true." It's not clear how mathematics leads to AI, so we will start with a philosophical framework.

The "WHAT-HOW-TOOLBOX Matrix of Reality" Is a Philosophical Framework

MIND-WHAT	EXTENSION-WHAT
MIND-HOW	EXTENSION-HOW
MIND-TOOLBOX	EXTENSION-TOOLBOX

Figure 1. Six boxes representing two attributes of reality in three divisions.

MIND-WHAT

Since artificial intelligence for the most part seems to be concerned with mental operations, in the first place let us discuss the nature of the mind and make some comments about *what* the mind is doing. This section discusses the so-called "MIND-WHAT" box in the matrix of figure 1. (Each box will be discussed in turn.) Some of these issues have been touched on above. Turing computation is mentioned again as it relates to mind. This section is not a comprehensive description of mind, but rather an attempt to emphasize certain more or less obvious points in relation to the AI framework.

The thinking activity itself does not seem to operate in any manner which we can associate with physical extension in space. It seems inherently immaterial, like a ghost in a building. It may seem that thought is spatial because it resides within the skull. That is true, and using modern fMRI techniques we can determine which parts of the brain are working during some given mental activity, thus thought is spatial in a certain sense. But it is *thought*

*considered from the perspective of active users of thought
- the qualia perspective -* that is of concern to us now.
We are concerned at this stage with the immediate
presentation and activity of thought, not the underlying
neural activities that seems to generate it.

Thus, in this framework we will consider mind non-spatial
in the tradition of Descartes.

Mind Integrates into a Single Totality

Mind integrates into a single totality whatever can be
experienced or thought, be it individual or multiple
immaterial ideas, sensations, emotions, memories, etc.
The whole is presented to and includes an I, with a simple
overall form "I think X," a well-trod template used by
philosophers. Here it is implied that X is some
understood proposition.

In the first place, simply put, there seems to be a single
unified totality of present experience within which
discrete thoughts and sensations can exist. We deal with
a totality of internal ideas and sensations which are
presented to and manipulated by an I instance. That
sensations are derived chiefly from external phenomena
does not of course change the fact that such internal
sensations are part of the mind's totality of thought.

Emotions seem to often stand somewhere in-between a
sensation and an overall idea. We can provisionally say
that an idea would include such components as emotions,
sensations, and memories.

The main point at this juncture, however, is the notion
that mind is wholly and completely integrated and
presented to a single person. Every idea that a mind can
think or sensation that it receives or emotion experienced
operates within these constraints. No thought is separate
from I. Every thought seems to be of the same form, "I
think X," which means we cannot just experience X - what
is thought is thought by an I.

Even though thought is unified in the I, at the same time,
obviously we are capable of having discrete thoughts which
are usually accompanied by an understanding. In many
cases a sensation is directly accompanied by a derived

idea. Differing emotions can spring up fairly
predictably.

Initially we can see that mind experiences a single,
immaterial, integrated totality at the same time that it
distinguishes components of the totality by directing its
attention accordingly. For example a memory can be
recollected so that it can be compared to some current
visual sensation. The result is that we experience the
visual sensation at the same instant as we experience the
memory, and the effect is that we experience a single
thing: a combination of a visual sensation and a memory.
Possibly an emotion is also experienced. Again, what we
experience are not discrete mental elements, such as
standalone sense, memory, reasoning, and emotional pieces
but an integrated, completely packaged result which we
could provisionally say is an *idea*.

It is amazing that the mind appears perfectly at ease
integrating seemingly discrete and immaterial components
of thought into a single idea. The immaterial nature of
mind appears at first as a sort of processing prerequisite
needed for the kind of mental integrations described above
(e.g., the integrated thought resulting from combining
visual sensation and memory).

Intuitively - to begin with at least - it is difficult to
envision an alternate three dimensional mind occupying
spatial reality working more or less like an immaterial
human mind. We tend to consider the mind as immaterial
and if we suddenly envision a three-dimensional machine
combining memories and sensations it may seem very strange
to us. A three dimensional mind extended in space with
integrated thoughts based upon memories, reasoning, sense
impressions, emotions, etc., seems to seriously violate
the essential definition of a mind so much so that we
might even recoil at the very idea, it seeming so
unnatural. Such is the difficult nature of AI.

Intuitively it does seem that the nature of mind as a non-
spatial thing means that the laws that apply to the
physical world of extension are not completely applicable
to mind, or at the very least it is not clear how physical
laws apply to mind. The concept of a boundary, in the
general context of metaphysics, to return to this example,
is well defined in the physical world but takes on a much
different meaning in the mental world, as described above.
It does seem for example that one thought can be separated
from another thought, and thus a kind of mental boundary

can be said to exist. We know that Socrates was a man.
We know that all men are mortal. Thus we know that
Socrates was mortal. Boundaries do seem to exist between
these thoughts - here sorts of boundaries divide the
premises and conclusion of a syllogism - in our mind.
But at the same time we seem to be able to break down the
mental boundary dividing each premise and see the entire
syllogism as a single integrated idea. It's as if we can
see through our mental boundaries so much so that there is
no boundary. There both is and isn't separation of the
individual premises that make up that syllogism. The
point here is that there is a serious question as to how
familiar concepts taken from physical reality apply to
mind.

Integrated Mental Input and Output

There evidently exists a single integrated present
external experience manifold including sensations and
actions used make input and output abstractions.

How does the mind interact with the world external to it?
We would have very limited lives indeed without a means of
interacting with the rest of the world. This is a very
important issue, and the relevant concepts of input and
output (I/O) were discussed a bit above.

From our computational background it is easy to use an
analogy of computer input and output as it relates to our
experience. Our long experiences with computing devices
tell us that data coming into a machine constitutes input
and conversely data being transmitted out falls under the
heading of output. The point is that there are two simple
avenues that some independent entity, be it a machine or a
person, interacts with the rest of the world: input and
output. We can easily envision a sound coming into the
ear as input, for example, and conversely the hand tapping
a table as output.

Some subtle differences between mind I/O and machine I/O
quickly become evident, however.

It is easy to envision the Turing machine's tape as an
ordinary data file containing program inputs and outputs
of the sort we are used to dealing with in typical
computer science. The tape, in other words, essentially
contains data being updated by an ordinary program.

The basic process of the Turing machine is to *input* a symbol from a specific location on the tape, and then based upon the symbol and the machine's present state alter the symbol, if necessary, with an *output* operation. Next the Turing machine updates its state and shifts to an adjacent symbol location on the tape. Then it starts this cycle of discrete steps over by input of the different symbol in the adjacent location.

It seems that the experience of mind in the physical world, on the other hand, does not present such crisp, discrete steps. Suppose I decide to "output" some speech, such as simply saying "hello world." The moment I output "hello world," the phrase is immediately input to me, presenting an experience that *output and input are one in the same thing*. In other words if I were akin to a Turing machine I would need something like an atomic write-and-read operation.

Suppose as another example I happen to be driving my car. As an analogy to a Turing machine, I am reading the transitions on the highway like symbols on a tape. Since I am driving, I am also altering the tape with output symbols. The problem is that we would need to introduce something like an atomic read-and-write operation so I could both read the contents of the tape, the state of the highway, and concurrently write to somewhere else on the tape my output commands to move the wheel.

Criticisms of the Turing machine are nothing new to AI. These are just a couple of points most relevant to this book. The main point is that the human analogs to discrete Turing machine operations present as integrated and concurrent.

It was claimed above that mind integrates into a single totality all that is experienced and thought, be it memories, emotions, reasonings, sensations, etc. It seems natural to presume that one aspect of this totality relates entirely to our present experience in the world. By "present experience in the world" I mean the manifold of present sensations and perceptions (as well as such thoughts directly attributable) whether caused in any way by some physical action ordered by the mind or not.

We all know people who are absent-minded. It is plainly possible to entertain complicated thinking that is virtually disconnected from our "present experience in the world." We can to a fairly high degree simply tune out our sensations and perceptions caused by our present experience in the world. Some people are better at this than others.

Suppose we provisionally divide the mind's single totality of thought into two aspects: one aspect being due to present experience in the world and the other aspect being such thinking taking place more or less completely divorced from present experience, i.e., the sort of thinking the absent-minded person busies himself with. Call it the "absent-minded division of thought."

This seems like a reasonable division, although nevertheless a matter of degree. Even the most absent-minded day dreamer, for example, would be likely to respond to the present sensation of a loud fire alarm. For the moment, though, forget about the part of our thinking that takes place in the "absent-minded division of thought." The primary issue at present is how we are to account for the mind's inputs from and outputs to the world external to it. Input and output are such fundamental issues in all of computer science and AI. The point is that in mind there appears to be a seemingly separable present experience manifold which is simply all input to the "I."

The mind can plainly cause change in the input present experience manifold. If I strike a light switch off, for example, the light intensity has been reduced in my input present experience manifold. My mind has *output* a command to switch a light off. But that doesn't make output a simple, discrete, disconnected opposite of input, as writing a symbol to tape is the opposite of reading a symbol on tape. It does mean that an alteration in the input to I occurs due to I's output command. Thus it is more like the input present experience manifold is first and foremost a substrate for cause and effect. Output we associate with causing changes that affect the input: output commands from the I, such as commands to move limbs, for example, change the input present experience manifold.

The notion of a manifold regarding integrated thinking is critical in Kant's philosophy, as detailed in his *Critique of Pure Reason* in which Kant also discusses the relevance

of "I think." The science of the inseparable nature of
input and output is of course nothing new, being central
to closed loop feedback theories studied in cybernetics.

Now-State in Now-Time

The mind experiences alterations of "now-state" of a goal
in "now-time."

Augustine of Hippo gave a legendary and straightforward
account of time in his *Confessions,* writing that "the mind
expects, it attends, and it remembers."[13] Thus regardless
of whether one happens to be expecting something, dealing
with a present occurrence, or reviewing memories, one is
invariably always limited just to the present moment in
time.

He hit on an idea that is so simple that you wonder if
he's missing something. It does seem that at least we can
be in all three states at once, to some degree, in an
endless transition. If I am presently watching a
quarterback prepare to throw a football, I remember the
last pass he threw and am expecting the upcoming pass to
be about the same quality. Yet, as Augustine notes, in
any case I am still in the present time.

Although physics does not yet give us a determinate
definition of time as we perceive it in the present, we
can still call this present time the "now-time." There is
never anything other than right now. The perception of
now-time seems to proceed basically in conjunction with
wall clock time.

The now-time in the first place is inherent in all aspects
of thought. Even static notions such as those found in
mathematics can only be thought in the present. Now-time
governs such basic thoughts as the expectation of eventual
death. I am aware of my eventual death right now, in the
present. I am aware of the event of my birth, obviously
in the past, but I am again only aware of this event in
the present. Whatever I am aware of I am aware of right
now.

Now-time can most readily be understood as it relates to a
belief about a discrete event. An event has a start, an
existence, and has either ended or the outcome is unknown,

32

although possibly may have strong likelihoods for its outcome. We may not have witnessed an event, but if it exists it had a start. If you are presently walking down the sidewalk and you see your friend John in a restaurant dining you know – at present – that he started this dining event in the past and it will end in the future. The belief that you have about John's dinner in now-time intrinsically contains an understanding about the event's beginning *and* ending.

Closely allied with time passage and the continual flow of events are changing mental states. When we say "mental state" it conjures up images of a person's emotional state, resisting precise definition. "Propositional attitude" concerns mental state in relation to some specific proposition, including the belief about the truth or falsity of a proposition. "Mental state" can also simply refer to whatever it feels like to think about something. When Turing talked about state he meant it to be analogous to some specific point a person is at in a scripted computational procedure.

We have then a fairly extensive muddle of things to think about when we refer to mental states. True, humans do seem to have frequently definable mental states, but plainly specific states and their transitions are not as tidy as a computer's bitwise state transitions.

In AI we are usually trying to do something, meaning that we are devising machines that attempt to reach some goal, be it win a chess game, safely disarm a dangerous bomb, etc. In the context of this framework then it seems reasonable to make this definition of mental state: those thoughts and feelings which vary at different stages of progress in the pursuit of a purposive goal. Obviously when we say "different stages of progress" we imply different times. There would be a mental state, for example, that accompanies the start of a chess game and another that accompanies the end of the game.

But it seems that the mental state at the end of the game is not altogether completely different than the mental state when the game started. It is more like the mental state at the end of the game is the transformation of the initial starting mental state; to a great extent the end mental state *is* the initial mental state. The goal of winning the game, regardless of outcome, pervades all mental states.

The realization of all but the most trivial of goals means that certain events need to take place. If I set a goal of doing the laundry, for example, the essential events would include gathering the clothes to be washed, putting detergent in the machine, executing the wash cycle, moving the clothes to the dryer, running the dryer, and then placing the clothes in some convenient location for use later.

For each of these steps, again, I can only think in the present. Thus if I am presently gathering the clothing I am also presently aware of the other steps in the future. By the time I am running the dryer I am also presently aware of having run the washer, now in the past.

My present beliefs about each of these events undergoes a transformation in now-time, seemingly in harmony with wall-clock time, each belief inherently containing the understanding of what has happened or what may happen. If I am presently executing the wash cycle I am presently aware of having put the detergent in the machine in the past and am presently aware of the need to move the clothing from the washing machine to the dryer in the future.

If I have already completed washing the clothes, the now-state of this event, washing the clothes, would be complete by virtue of now-time telling me that it is presently in the past.

The now-state of a goal we can think of as the result of correlating all the beliefs about events needed to reach the goal.

In our example, the now-state of the main goal, doing the laundry, indicates "in-progress" if I am presently running the dryer. The now-state of the main goal is itself in now-time. This means that the understanding we have about the main goal in the present contains past, present, and future information about *each event*, or equivalently sub-goal, needed to complete the main goal: the now-state of the main goal is made up of the now-states of each sub-goal needed to complete the main goal.

The concepts of now-state and now-time saturate all beliefs regarding events. Our understanding of a goal in a now-state seems to inherently contain all relevant past and future states by virtue of the characteristic now-time.

This scheme makes the situation strikingly different from Turing computation. No one would say that the present state in a Turing machine is not just its present state but also its past states and future states. Yet, in a human mental state we seem to easily accommodate past, present, and possible future states under the auspices of a single present state. The transformation rate of state of mind seems to take place in a commonsense realm of time flow which is not set up simply to run as quickly as possible like a computer. Rather, now-time seems to be in harmony with the unfolding of more or less natural events.

Motivations Drive Goal-Oriented Behavior

Much has been written about the relation of motivation to behavior. The Wikipedia encyclopedia[source online] defined motivation as follows:

> "Motivation is the psychological feature that arouses an organism to action toward a desired goal and elicits, controls, and sustains certain goal directed behaviors. For instance: An individual has not eaten, he or she feels hungry, and as a response he or she eats and diminishes feelings of hunger. There are many approaches to motivation: physiological, behavioral, cognitive, and social. Motivation may be rooted in a basic need to minimize physical pain and maximize pleasure, or it may include specific needs such as eating and resting, or for a desired object. Conceptually, motivation is related to, but distinct from, emotion."

Psychology provides no indisputable and all-encompassing theory regarding motivation. However, it does seem self-evident that (very broadly stated) one's motivations spring simply from the twin pursuits of increasing pleasure and decreasing pain. Thus motivation seems driven by emotions. Alternately put, we want to increase the good in our lives – good meaning whatever it is that makes us feel better – and decrease the bad which we can define as what makes us feel worse. In a sense then, it does appear that motivation can be very simply defined and it seems to play an incredibly important role in life: without motivation nothing would ever happen, at least in the realm of human activity. The school of behaviorism, of course, is predicated upon these essential ideas.

Two of the most well known AI systems seem to start with a predefined goal provided by the system developers. IBM's *Deep Blue* has the goal of checkmate. IBM's *Watson* has the predefined goal of answering some query. The goals these programs have seem to be their root starting point. The entire issue of *why* these goals were pursued has nothing to do with the program in itself. The motivations for these programs were not experienced by the programs in question, but rather by the IBM executives that drove their development.

There does seem to be a chasm of sorts between a person's motivation and goal. A man has the emotional motivation of boredom. He sets a goal of taking in a show or indulging in a hobby. We don't appear to start with a goal, for example, such as "drive to the store and buy dinner." We would start rather with the motivation of "I'm hungry" and only then determine a goal intended to satisfy the motivation.

Of course, just because we can experience and envision motivations in a straightforward manner does not make for something immediately equivalent on a Turing machine. Formalizing the transformation of motivation to determinate goal is no small undertaking. The point here is to emphasize that motivations, with their fairly simple emotional drives essentially toward the twin good ends of increasing pleasure and decreasing pain, are the driving force of thinking human behavior – making the issue, usually omitted in AI, crucial.

The question, of course, of whether or not or to what extent we can control our motivations is closely allied to the notion of the *will*. Even though we may be strongly motivated to pursue a goal, we retain the power to choose – to will – among alternative actions.

The Mind Is Self-Organized

Each of us has the responsibility for organizing his own thinking. Aside from arguably the use of drugs, surgery, drastic measures like electroshock therapy, or injury

36

there is really no way of reaching into a person's head
and changing the way he thinks. (Science may ultimately
be able to do this, of course.)

A person's manner of thinking can obviously change; new
things can be learned, memories formed, habits acquired,
and so forth. However, this happens in a mysterious
manner not accessible to others. We can't program another
person's mind externally in a manner akin to programming a
computer. A person could still be "programmed," but the
connotation of the word in this case means some (generally
undesired) manipulation taking place externally. There is
no natural way of reaching into a man's head and altering
his neural networks, for example, so that a new goal is in
place.

The mind is simply not programmed in the sense that we are
used to thinking of programming a computer, although it is
common to hear claims of the brain being a type of
computer. Plainly we can each be taught or invent
algorithms, procedures, rules, and the like, but we
organize our thinking in a manner not accessible to
others.

Of course, an important point of behaviorism is the
formalization of general observable external behavior
without attempting to determine a structure or
organization of internal thinking patterns. Behaviorism
has little to say about thought processes. Under
behaviorism the mind is regarded as a black box.
Artificial neural networks, a subfield within AI, function
essentially as black boxes, being in general trained with
patterns along a continuum, in either a supervised or
unsupervised fashion. Neural networks are not programmed
but trained. Like behaviorism with its de-emphasis of
thought function and structure, there is ultimately little
concern about how the neural network actually functions
internally.

In a certain sense behaviorism along with neural networks
represent a realistic approach to strong AI by emphasizing
the self-organizing aspect of mind. Can we ever be
completely assured of how someone else thinks?

The Content of Mind Is Ideas as Understood Propositions

We have already talked about ideas briefly above. An idea
as defined by Mario Bunge is "an umbrella term that
designates a percept, an image, a concept, a proposition,
a classification, a doctrine, a theory, or whatever else
can be thought. Because of such generality, it is hard to
conceive that there could be a single precise theory of
ideas of all kinds."[12]

An idea is rightly a general term but an idea seems to be
more like the *result* of *integrating* seemingly discrete
types, such as multiple percepts, images, concepts,
propositions, memories, etc. And it also is plainly
evident that strong emotions can influence, and thus be an
integral part of, ideas, yet philosophers rarely seem to
incorporate seemingly base emotions in idealist theories.
The question, which is certainly "hard to conceive" an
answer to, is how this generality of everything thinkable
– i.e., the idea – can ever be managed.

If everything thinkable is an idea, can *any* idea then be
put in a common form? Naturally, since we cannot (or at
least should not – present science is working on this)
read the ideas in someone else's mind, we need a common
communication form to express our ideas.

Philosophers have long made use of the propositional form
in logic. Of course, there is the ancient propositional
logic championed by the Stoics. There is also the equally
ancient Aristotelian logic which forms propositions by
affirming or denying a predicate of a subject. Clearly
philosophers have long envisioned propositions as the
fundamental means to convey and prove. There are various
formal definitions of *proposition*, but for the moment
consider a proposition as any ordinary meaningful
sentence.

Wittgenstein's famous *Tractatus Logico-Philosophicus*
includes a basic framework of reality.[14] The chief mental
component is the internal representation, the "picture,"
which we may as well take to be roughly equivalent to the
above working definition of idea. According to
Wittgenstein, importantly, we can further view a thought-
picture in terms of propositions.

Hegel, in his *Science of Logic,* in developing his objective logic, claims that "reflections," basically a building block of his ultimate idea, "already contain within themselves the propositional form."[15]

Even disregarding what these philosophers and others have concluded it seems safe to say that we can normally communicate most of our ideas using propositions. Furthermore we can usually summarize and compress even complicated ideas into a single sentence with an ordinary subject and predicate.

Note that we do not always describe our ideas with words. We could use body language to communicate. Perhaps we describe someone's attitude by a shrug of the shoulders. In this case the subject is the person in question and the communicated predicate something like "I don't know what to tell you." If it is a musical melody which constitutes our idea, we might hum the melody, or use the sheet music, describe a sequence of notes, or just pick up a guitar and play it. In this latter type of case the subject could be something like "the song I presently like" and the communicated predicate the contents of the song.

The propositional form always seems to be somehow evident when we have something in mind - that is when we have any arbitrary idea. Perhaps I am thinking the sun is going to come out this weekend. Maybe I am thinking that I've had too much caffeine. Maybe I am thinking of what Jimi Hendrix sounded like. Maybe I am thinking of what pizza tastes like. In any case with any idea there seems to always be a subject along with whatever I am associating with the subject - that is the predicate. I understand these propositions, they mean something to me, and they have a subject-predicate structure. These constants appear to hold whether I happen to translate an idea into language or not.

Now, it seems that understanding an idea is so important it may as well be the central point of the discussion of an idea. Indeed, an *idea seems to be simply that which is understood.* Just because we can put an idea forth in a seemingly simple subject-predicate proposition does not directly lead to an understanding, and therein lies a fundamental problem with AI.

In traditional computer science suppose we see a payroll system proposition: "John Doe has a salary of $50,000."

"John Doe" is the subject and "has a salary of $50,000" the predicate. Perhaps we can construct a Prolog program with the term "salary(JohnDoe,50000)," salary here being considered the predicate in Prolog.

But that sort of approach doesn't net anything like an *understanding* of an idea. The understanding that someone has about "John Doe's salary" is *something else that escapes present forms of definition.*

When someone says that "John Doe's salary is $50,000" I understand what is meant but in reality I have no idea how I understand it. True, I could say that I understand what salary means, what payments are, who "John Doe" is, and how these factors together lead to *my* understanding of his salary, but that is only a potentially infinite regress of grounds for my understanding, but not an adequate description of actually understanding.

Understanding is a strange thing. What does it mean to say we *understand*? Sometimes I picture Dennis Hopper's spaced-out photographer character in the last scenes of the great film *Apocalypse Now* waiving his arms wildly in fits of metaphysics. What do you mean by "understand" man?

Of course the AI community has been asking essentially the same question, somewhat more soberly, generally under the heading of the "symbol grounding problem." Here we seek to define how internal symbols such as those manipulated in an ordinary computer could ever come to accurately mean something.

We often understand that we don't understand some idea. Not understanding an idea is a sort of understood idea in its own right. In any case it can still be put in a sort of positive form by saying "I understand that I don't understand that."

How we understand ideas, how we can change ideas, how one idea may be superior to another, and all such matters are critical to AI. If there is a calculus possible for the realm of ideas remains to be seen and seems to rest on the symbol grounding problem. It may be what is required should more accurately be named a "calculus of the understandings."

Summary

In this section certain characteristics of mind were described. In summary, the mind presents a single integrated totality always in the simple form "I think X," X being some understood proposition by an I. There are subtle differences between machine and mind input/output, most notably that as a simple generalization everything experienced seems input to the mind. The present – the *now* – is of critical importance as mental state is always limited to the present time. Motivations, not generally addressed by AI, are also of critical importance, seeming to be the root source of all behavior. While software is generally programmed by a human, a mind is essentially a black box. Thus learning takes place in an overwhelmingly mysterious way, not readily accessible to others. Finally, an idea seems to be *that which is understood*, and it presents in a general subject-predicate propositional form. We truly do not know how we understand ideas. While we can cite various grounds to support our understanding of individual ideas, it leads to an infinite regress of grounds for understanding – each a contributing factor itself *already understood*. Nevertheless, we can usually translate ideas into a form immediately intelligible to others, be it using language, gestures, sounds, etc.

MIND-HOW

This book takes the simple standpoint that whatever it is that constitutes thought in a readily available form presented to and a part of a person falls under the so-called MIND-WHAT: simply *what* the mind is doing for a user. Certain characteristics were covered above in MIND-WHAT and fall generally under the heading of consciousness. Whatever it is that makes that happen – that is, makes consciousness happen – belongs in the "HOW" component in the matrix, here the so-called MIND-HOW. This creates a demarcation line. Another way to think of this division is that MIND-WHAT falls roughly under the heading of psychology and MIND-HOW roughly under the heading of neuroscience.

The Problem is We Don't Really Know How the Brain Works

Let us take an example to illustrate this distinction. Suppose you want to examine a photograph of a friend. You instantly recognize him, although let us say that perhaps his face is only partly shown. How is it that you recognized him? It is true that you can say "I recognized him because I have seen his face before and it is retrieved from my memory." True, but that is a description of *what* happened and not *how* it happened (at least under the divisions established herein). You are aware of remembering his face. You may have made an effort to remember him, but that still does not explain how you remembered, only that you expended an effort to remember.

Even if you said "I remember his face when I think of soccer players" and hence your mind operated by association, still you don't have to operate such an association "manually": no awareness of actual chemical activity in the brain, no attention given to the firing of neurons, no effort expended upon the mysterious translation of this neurally derived similarity into *beliefs* – none of these things are accessed by you when recognizing a friend in a picture.

Suppose we take another example, such as the mind's execution of any ordinary syllogism. True, we can describe the steps taken, terms used, major premise, minor premise, conclusion, etc. But again, these steps constitute a characterization of what is happening, that is the conscious experience of a syllogism, not how the syllogism is happening (again, at least in the context of falling under the distinctions we are going to adhere to).

Basically no one has a definite answer to the question of how the mind works – we just have a pretty good assemblage of the parts involved by taking into consideration the considerable contributions of the various fields including philosophy, psychology, neuroscience, AI, and others (the trend these days is to hybridize these fields, such as "computational neuroscience"). This book seeks to identify some major characteristics of how the mind works, not provide a definitive explanation.

It is hardly necessary for us to know how the brain creates thought as day-to-day "users." Thankfully we are relieved of the necessity of actually operating our minds beyond simply expending the effort to think something, and again every thought is of the simple form "I think X."

This convenient setup however makes it quite problematic to construct a machine for the thinking activity because evolution crafted the mind to be free of access to important operational details for the sake of comparative ease of use.

Functionally, we know we have an attentive facility, memories, sense impressions, reasoning, perceptive abilities, means of commanding motion from our bodies, emotions, and so forth. All of these functions have a way of working together. We know we have memory since otherwise it would be impossible to remember, perception since we can identify things in groups, and so on. We have inferred these multiple constituent parts of mind and identified certain causative aspects in the brain via neuroscience. Neuroscience, having at least roughly mapped the architecture of the brain, can tell us for example that when we enjoy music certain areas of the brain are activated. When we see certain visual patterns certain neurons fire. Neuroscience in this age is hot on the trail for answers to these types of questions and the separation between the respective fields of psychology and neuroscience is shrinking.

Returning to our example of recognizing a friend in a picture, we could, for example, say that neuroscience tells us that memories are stored in a certain set of cells, arranged in a certain fashion, and that certain parts of the brain are activated in your retrieving this memory. Psychology could tell us about your long term memory, episodic memory, short term memory, and so forth. Modal logic could provide a formalism for reasoning temporally about events around the time of the picture. Other fields, such as sociology and linguistics, for example, could be brought into play.

From these various perspectives we can then characterize the mind's operation in various ways. Yet, simply put: short of a major breakthrough there still is no completely adequate, unified description of how the mind works. We can form reasonable ideas about it, but we still aren't "there" yet with an overarching, comprehensive model. Psychology, neuroscience, mathematics, related fields, and hybrid related fields each offer some description of how the mind or brain works. Yet we are still left with an

incomplete feeling, the sort of feeling we might get about
hearing a friend talking about a trip somewhere.

Suppose your friend has just returned from a trip to
Paris. He has pictures, videos, documents, brochures,
descriptions of sightseeing, and wild tales of nights on
the town. Yet no matter how detailed the description, it
is just that, a description of different aspects of the
trip. It is fun to listen to. Yet, it seems to you that
no matter how detailed the description of the trip,
hearing about a trip to Paris and actually going there are
not the same thing. The ideas you conjure up as a result
of the friend's description are a varied jumble. Some
incidents are left incomplete, stories from various other
friends are included haphazardly. Some incidents seem to
be greatly exaggerated. You try to fill in the blanks.
Different accounts of Parisian incidents seem biased in
some way. You hear about impressive museums, art nouveau
subway stops, the Eiffel Tower, the food, the poodles.
But how are these different aspects of the trip put
together to yield some sort of overall impression?
Curiosity remains. You have an idea about what it is
like to go to Paris, but you still haven't been there.
You are still left to your own ideas as far as how to
relate these descriptions of Paris to what Paris is really
like. You decide you actually need to go to Paris,
because otherwise all you have to work with is a set of
various descriptions.

With respect to the question of how the mind works, it is
like we haven't yet been to Paris. We have no complete
overarching theory. We just have lots of different
accounts.

But that does not stop us from pointing out some basic
ideas about how the mind works. Perhaps we haven't yet
"gone to Paris" but we can still talk intelligibly about
certain aspects of it.

It should also be noted that as of 2013 two notable large
scale, ten year projects are underway to meet this
challenge: the BRAIN Initiative (Brain Research through
Advancing Innovative Neurotechnologies) based in the
United States, and the Human Brain Project supported in
the European Union.

Device Independence

As mentioned above, the mind does seem to operate with no awareness of *how* it operates. This seems to be a very important issue: the seeming virtual "device independence" that takes place. We describe software as device independent if it can run on any applicable hardware. The effect rendered in our context herein is that the mind rests on the illusion of separability and indifference to whatever brain wetware that is "running it."

This setup of course provides the grounds for endless arguments regarding the separable nature of soul and body, but the point here is that the result is a *seeming* independence of the mind from its wetware brain, not to engage in debates regarding any actual independence of the mind from the wetware brain.

One of the major factors then in how the mind works is the issue of seeming "device independence." Some wetware brain is working to create some mind. Without this realized "device independence" it is difficult to imagine the mind as we know it.

The most remarkable aspect of the effective "device independence" of the mind is arguably that of the attendant integrated nature of mind – that the assemblage of brain structures and mechanisms somehow creates a *single immaterial, independent mind*.

The General Understanding and Belief Generator

Another characteristic of how the mind works is that the brain's wetware seems to act as a "general understanding/belief generator." I see the coffee mug in front of me. I have an idea that the coffee mug is in front of me. I understand immediately that the mug is in front of me. I seem to have full access to the idea that the mug is in front of me, but I don't have access to how I know the mug is in front of me, other than to state that I see it. But seeing a mug in front of me is not quite the same thing as understanding that there is a mug in front of me. More is required.

A memory of a coffee mug has to be dealt with. The smell of coffee may be needed. I have to understand that a mug is not part of my body. But even if we explain the various grounds we use in understanding a coffee mug in front of us, in this example by identifying its shape and smelling its contents, there still is a serious question (as discussed in the above MIND-WHAT section) as to how we tie these grounds together and produce what constitutes an understanding of the situation. The understanding seems to take place entirely behind the scenes and is something that seems to escape present forms of science.

Again, what exactly happens when we understand? In the age that we live in we deal constantly with symbolic formalisms in programming which describe some aspect of a situation, arrived at by the constraints implicit in abstraction. It is hard to think of representing any problem without recourse to some programmable, abstract, symbolic representation.

We can design a program to recognize a coffee cup. But when we say "I understand there is a coffee cup in front of me" there seems to be no straightforward means as to how to formalize such an ordinary and everyday occurrence. Yes, we can write a program to recognize coffee cups. This can be grounded in the appearance of typical coffee cups. But we don't have ready access to whatever it is that allows us to understand coffee cups. In short human understanding and symbolic programmable manipulations seem to be much different things.

To illustrate this problem, suppose we say the word "experience." We know what experience means, but we don't know how we know what experience means, other than we could possibly remember when we learned what it meant. But that only means we recall that we learned it. It doesn't account for how we learned the word or how we understand it. The understanding seems to be hidden from us.

In terms of the philosophical framework, when I say "understand" I mean that which renders an idea (as defined in the WHAT above) completely meaningful. True, we can strive to understand something, we can engage in thinking, imagining, and reasoning, but ultimately the understanding that we arrive at is fundamentally given to us but still a mystery to us. All that we can really do is describe whatever it is that led us to understand something, and whatever it entails, but we still cannot explain how we understand. In our example we know *what* "experience" means without knowing *how* we understand what it means.

There also seems to be a kind of system of belief that goes along with whatever I understand. I believe in all sorts of things. I believe in time and space. Usually my beliefs about reality seem to be confirmed with some sort of evidence. If I see daylight outside then I believe it is day, otherwise I believe it is night. Whatever I regard as true about reality seems to be essentially a belief about reality.

It is for these reasons it can be claimed that the brain is fundamentally a mysterious "general understanding/belief generator" for our ideas. Understandings and beliefs seem to go hand in hand. We gain understandings of fairly discrete ideas backed up by a system of beliefs that collectively contribute to the idea.

The Mental Megafunction

There seems to be quite a few things at the disposal of our will. For example, I can will myself to add numbers, move my eyes, to speak, to think critically, to remember, and so on. Whenever I will something, be it simple like remembering what day it is, or somewhat harder, like doing my taxes, I seem to use basically the same method: for whatever I will I call a single "megafunction." The megafunction seems to accept whatever specific function I require along with arguments needed to fill the request.

There is something gloriously simple about this setup. Whatever I will, I happily just call the same megafunction. Period. Or at least it seems that way. When I declare "I will X" it is like saying "I call my megafunction with argument X."

If I have the idea of wanting to remember how to play a chord on the guitar I will so and call my mental megafunction with the argument to remember a chord. My original idea of wanting to remember a guitar chord has been mysteriously transformed into the memory of a chord. If I will that my hand moves I again call my single megafunction with the argument to move my hand. If I want to imagine a pink elephant car wash, again, I call the same megafunction with the arguments in question. Now I can envision a pink elephant car wash. The megafunction simply returns an understanding without any indication of how it arrived at it.

Possibly the understanding returned by the megafunction includes a different emotion, an image, or a physical motion, such as speech, or even a request for missing information. Possibly the megafunction cannot process my request, so it might return "don't understand."

Let us take more examples. Suppose I have the idea that I want to add some numbers. That is *what* I have in mind: my idea of adding a specific list of numbers. I understand what this means at the outset, with the "how" of my mind supplying the understanding and belief that I want to add a given list of numbers.

I understand and believe that I want to add some numbers. Truly I probably don't even know how I understand that I want to add some numbers. In general it seems that all we really have are our ideas and the will to change them. At any rate, next I call my single megafunction with the request to add some numbers along with the list of numbers. Soon I understand the answer to my arithmetic question. My original idea has been altered – in a way that I don't quite understand – conveniently giving me a result. My original idea was "I will to add this list of numbers." Now that I know the answer, I could claim that the original idea of simply wanting to add numbers had been superseded by the answer, itself an idea. My idea has been altered.

The moment we probe ourselves into how we understand an idea, we only uncover more ideas. If I ask myself how I can add two numbers, true, I remember doing it in elementary school, I can think of lining numbers up in a column and so forth, but that only reveals more ideas about arithmetic. There still seems to be, again, *no indication of how I understand this*. It seems that how we understand ideas can only be characterized. I understand my ideas but I don't understand how I understand my ideas. I can formalize how I understand ideas, for example with logic, but that is not the same thing as understanding.

So we seem to have a virtual single megafunction at our disposal which we call for whatever we will. It seems to return an understanding, or a not-understanding with requests for more details.

Suppose I drop a pen and pick it up. The initial idea is
that I understand that the pen slipped out of my hand and
I heard it hit the floor. Then I seem to understand the
idea that I need to find it. Next I understand the idea
that I don't know where it is. I may have the fear that I
have lost a special pen given for participating in a
wedding. This too I understand. Hence at this point I
could apprehensively say "I have no idea where my pen
went." This idea seems to be accompanied by the
understanding that I will need to look for it, and if it
is not behind the desk it is to the side of it. I check
to the side of the desk, understand that it is not there,
then check behind the desk, and understand that it is
there and pick it up.

My original idea, "I've lost my pen" has by now been
significantly altered to "I've picked up my pen." We see
a fairly smooth transition from the original lost-pen idea
to a looking-for-pen idea, and finally to found-pen idea.
At the same time, it seems that what I have done is
processed essentially a *single changing idea*, call it
lost-and-found-my-pen, that came complete with sense
impressions, requests for missing information, commands to
move my body, and an overall understanding of the
situation and how it developed.

The understanding/belief-generating megafunction then
seems to accompany my ideas at all times – providing their
changing understandings. I simply do not know *how* I
understand *what* I understand but when I seek to understand
under the right circumstances *what ideas* I have I
understand.

The megafunction seems to return an understanding as best
it can for whatever *I will*, including it would seem an
understanding of the will itself. The megafunction seems
to be able to provide an understanding of ideas which are
themselves possibly subcomponents or dimensions of an
overall idea. The megafunction seems to be able to return
values of true or false. It seems to also return
"understand" or "don't understand, need more information."
It also seems to return "understand, and did you also
think of this associated issue?"

The megafunction may also return an understanding when I
don't invoke it by will, as for instance when someone taps
me on the shoulder: I have an instant understanding of

the idea that someone is tapping me on the shoulder. The
megafunction appears to be able to gain new knowledge so
that on successive calls it does not need to return "don't
understand, need more information."

The megafunction provides emotions along with virtually
all ideas. If somebody is rushing at me with an ax I am
seized by considerable alarm. I fully understand the
alarm. Thus the understanding coming along with an idea
like this would be accompanied by a sense of priority.

The following are examples of invoking the megafunction:
"Remember Becky," remembering; "the king can only move one
square," learning; "where is my friend in the crowd?"
perceiving; "Is Paris the capital of France?" deciding
true or false. We associate verbs with these megafunction
calls: remembering, learning, perceiving, deciding, etc.

The megafunction, in supplying an understanding for all
our ideas, has at its disposal roughly all of the elements
of psychology: attention, perception, various types of
memory, knowledge, sensations, language, and so forth.

The megafunction may not return anything useful, or may
not be able to supply an understanding, or it may supply a
partial or inadequate understanding, but, again, it does
seem that when we don't understand something, we have the
understanding that we don't understand. Hence it seems
that some form of understanding accompanies any thought –
even if the understanding is "I don't understand."

The core of thinking seems to be a constant interaction
between the will, ideas, and understanding, *each aspects
of a singular whole.*

Suppose I see a new word in an article. I read the word
and have in mind an understanding of an idea of the word
in question, but my understanding tells me that I don't
know what the word means, i.e., my megafunction returned
"don't understand." My will seems to be invoked because I
desire to learn new words at this point based upon my
understanding of not understanding the word. My idea has
shifted to wanting to learn the new word since I don't
know it. So I look up the word, but at first I still
don't understand it, so my will again invokes my
megafunction, which hopefully eventually returns an
understanding of the idea of the meaning of the new word

after scrutinizing the definition and some examples. The
will, idea, and understanding of this event seem to
smoothly interact and change in now-time.

Like the Components of a Machine Operating Together in Time

What is presented to me in my mind is a single integrated
totality, and research shows that there is indeed a
staggering level of interconnection in the brain.
Obviously, however, it is clear (at the physical level)
the brain is still composed of fairly discrete components
connected together.   In general neuroscience tells us
that we have a very high level of interconnection between
discrete parts of the brain. It seems fair to say that
the design of the brain is as both discrete and connected.

It should be no surprise then given the discrete-and-
connected nature of the brain that we think such that we
can form discrete ideas, but ideas never seem to be
totally in isolation. If a man suddenly charged at me
wielding an ax, my visual centers (which are known to be
spread throughout the brain) are activated, then I fear,
then possibly I try to make a threat. We see here what
appears to be an interaction of discrete parts of a whole.
Vision, fear, and threat seem to be markedly different
things, and probably originate in different parts of the
brain, but there is incontestably a certain predictability
and structure apparent in how these different mental
components interact. We seem to see what appears to be
similar to components of a machine operating together in
time.

Summary

So, to summarize, how do we characterize *how* the mind
works? In the first place brain wetware generates an
integrated mind, which basically consists of immaterial
ideas. The mind has a real or virtual "device
independence" property, seeming to be separate and almost
indifferent to the brain "running it." We can, using
will, arbitrarily seek to understand our changing ideas by
calls to the single megafunction, which supplies an
understanding (or supplies the understanding of not
understanding). We can characterize the understandings of
ideas we have but we still truly do not know how we
understand - we just understand. There are discrete-yet-

connected mental structures operating in time in a manner akin to a physical machine.

MIND-TOOLBOX

In this section of the matrix we concern ourselves with the sciences applicable to mind – we can informally call this section then a "toolbox" of sorts. Imagine that an ultimate toolbox could be used to construct a brain. At this point, however, we need to content ourselves with present science.

The thought issues described above under the MIND-WHAT and MIND-HOW sections are characterized by a high level of integration: ideas that we have seem present as a part of a single integrated totality. When we understand an idea we seem to have an awareness, however unconsciously, of related issues, and our minds integrate many issues and beliefs easily. Even though we can say that we may have two ideas, for instance, there is still only a single I for which the ideas are integrated. What has been attempted in the above sections is a characterization of this integrative phenomenon from the standpoint of what is happening in the mind and how it is happening and we can safely claim that no matter how diverse our ideas there is nevertheless integration into a single totality, I.

The problem is that, in general, while this section of the toolbox concerns science, not enough progress has been made in the area of mental integration, this issue known generally as the questions surrounding the "binding problem." Equally problematic is that consciousness seems to be spread out into multiple disciplines, each creating its own partially overlapping sets of narrow rules. Abstraction, not integration, characterizes the sciences yet the mind is overwhelmingly integrated. An example will help.

Suppose you are at a dinner party and are shown a picture of yourself with a friend. This picture represents a small piece from your life. If we consider your life as a whole, let us say that the picture is an abstraction from that whole.

Looking at the picture you know that the picture was taken in the past since pictures must represent something that has already happened, that you have a memory that it was sunny later in the day, that your friend is a colleague on equal standing with you, has a good attitude, that you were both dressed in now-outdated fashions, that you gained weight since then, and so on.

While your mind seems to have at its disposal abstracting tools that will produce these details, you can still take in the meaning of the photograph essentially at once as a single overall idea.

Just in this example scenario of looking at a picture, which we can consider an abstraction from the whole of your conscious life, we see a vast assortment of issues that represent further abstractions and could themselves be isolated and studied in psychology, philosophy, sociology, and probably other fields. A "good attitude" could fall under psychology, the fact that a picture already taken must represent something that has already happened, formalized under temporal logic in philosophy, the issues of gaining weight and having a colleague could fall under the study of sociology. These individual fields of study describe some of the laws, principles, theorems, processes, and so on applicable to the idea at hand.

We seem to continue down a kind of hierarchy of abstraction. In the first place we said that the picture represented an abstraction if we consider your life as a whole. Now given the picture we can continue abstracting and studying its constituent parts. We seem to continually be separating and studying some property or piece extracted from its whole. Science does well in this scenario, that is of classifying and creating rules that can later be applied generally, so long as we properly constrain the situation under consideration. As mentioned, sociology would have something to say about gaining weight and its effect on social status as a general rule. This could be applied to the situation. But in order to fully process the situation you also need to recognize your friend, and this is a memory issue, under psychology.

The net problem is that there is no adequate integrative field, only various different fields that can describe various aspects from various perspectives of various situations of conscious experience. Such is the intent of virtually all science and the epitome of the problem of narrow, not general and integrated AI.

This is still useful, of course. Each of these fields and
others do provide us with a toolbox of sorts to work with.
We are great at extracting useful properties from overall
concepts and situations because we are so good at managing
context. We know what properties are relevant in
different situations and these are the properties
extracted and studied.

Summary

In summary, the relatively isolated study of abstractions
applicable to mind we shall say constitutes its "toolbox,"
at least in this day, and these are the issues that
largely fall under philosophy, psychology, and related
fields each considered in isolation. These fields
describe the discrete rules and laws applicable to their
respective domain, are somehow applicable to the way we
think, but generally provide sort of atomic, narrow
building blocks of some part of thought without describing
how the end result, an idea, is integrated and thus
achieved. There is not enough in this cumulative toolbox
to construct an integrative mental totality.

We are impressed but left with the distinct feeling of
being left with a lot of parts – and no whole.

EXTENSION-WHAT

We now turn from mind to physical reality. Extension was
the term used by Descartes to describe physical matter
extended in three dimensional space.

Philosophical dualisms, such as Descartes' mind and matter
dualism, are not particularly fashionable in the present
era. There is, however, a justification: we've had a
hard time creating strong AI with the tacit assumption
that mind and matter are essentially the *same thing,* the
implication being that the discovery of heretofore elusive
algorithms to run on a Turing machine is all that is
missing.   That is not to say that strong AI will be easy
if we just separate mind from matter in our framework, but
it does at least make the distinction plain in the hopes

54

that we can work out how mind and matter are the same, and
how different.

Coined Terms to Describe Physical Events

The following describes some simple coined terms that we
can use to characterize physical events. In the most
general sense, in the realm of Cartesian extension – the
physical world – if something is happening we can say
"something is happening," a very general way to describe
any occurrence while giving no indication of cause and
effect. If we want to account for more detail, every
something-is-happening can more specifically be described
in terms of what-is-happening and how-it-is-happening.
Something-is-happening is then a general term that
contains implicitly both what-is-happening and how-it-is-
happening.

If we take only a single component in physical space, in
isolation, nothing can be said to be happening. If the
universe happened to be filled with, for example, nothing
but a door handle, there would be nothing of consequence
that could be said about it. There would be nothing in
relation to the door handle. No door, no mechanical
assembly, just a simple unattached handle. In fact there
would be no grounds for saying that it was unattached
since something else would need to exist for the phrase to
have any meaning. About all that could be said is "there
is a door handle," if even that, since there would be no
one to make such a bold statement and the terms in the
prior paragraph would be essentially null.

With only a door handle in our starter universe nothing
would ever happen. Fortunately the universe contains more
than a single thing to work with. Interesting things
start to happen in the universe when two or more
components interact, combine, separate, and so forth. It
seems safe to make the humble claim that when two or more
components interact something-is-happening.

Here we won't precisely define "component" but informally
visualize it simply as some object in the three-
dimensional, physical universe which can potentiality
interact with other objects in the universe.

Let's expand our simple doorknob and use it in a simple
scenario in our present universe. If you turn the handle

the cylinder pulls in the direction of the turn. Ignoring some of the mechanical parts of lesser importance from this example, what we essentially have is the first component, the door handle, pulling the second component, the cylinder. At this point two components are interacting and we can say generally that something-is-happening.

Even at this stage, what-is-happening seems to be different from the action of the constituent components that are causing whatever it is that is happening. The door handle turning is causing the cylinder to move, but while this may involve two discrete components which can each be considered in isolated abstraction, namely the handle and the cylinder, there seems to be only a collective single thing happening – in simple terms we are retracting a latch (the cylinder portion which protrudes into the area of the door).

What-is-happening then at this point is "retracting a latch," and that is the integrated result of our two components interacting. To the question "what is happening?" we can safely answer "retracting a latch." To the question "how is 'retracting a latch' happening?" we can answer "the turning handle is causing the cylinder to move inward."

Continuing our example in a second step, let us introduce another component to our little system: the force of your arm pulling or pushing the door after you have turned its handle. Now to the question "what is happening?" you can respond, "opening the door." To the question "how is the door opening?" you can respond "because the latch was retracted and I am now pulling the handle."

Think in terms of the questions "what is happening?" and "how is it happening?"

In our first step the what-is-happening is "retracting a latch." But now in the second step the what-is-happening is generalized to simply "opening the door." The retracting latch from the first step is given as a cause to partially describe how the door is opening.

We shifted our *focal point* from thinking about the "latch retracting" as a what-is-happening to using the very same "latch retracing" as a cause of another what-is-happening, namely "opening the door." In this example a how-it-is-happening for "opening the door" includes a what-is-happening, "retracting a latch" and another what-is-happening, "pulling the handle."

Means and Ends

Another way of looking at this example is to consider a what-is-happening as purposive *ends* and how-it-is-happening as the *means* causing these purposive ends. Hence "latch retracting" is in the first instance the ends caused by means of the door handle pulling the cylinder. In the second instance the ends achieved, "opening the door" is based upon the means of "latch retracting," formerly considered the ends, and also by means of "pulling the handle."

We see a transformation of the *same* action considered as *ends* to being considered as *means* causing other additional ends. The ends from one stage of our example become the means in the next stage. The means cause the ends. We also see the cumulative nature of the what-is-happening. In our example, an overall something-is-happening is the physical event of a door opening. The something-is-happening subsumes a set of what-is-happenings, namely "retracting the latch" and "pulling the handle."

Propositional Form

Answers to the questions "what is happening" and "how is it happening" are already in proposition form.

It is amazing the degree to which we can summarize complicated scenarios in a single proposition. Suppose you see a NASA space rocket blasting off. You can say "there is a rocket blasting off" even though there are a massive number of subcomponents involved, or put in the terminology herein a massive number of what-is-happenings involved. If the main what-is-happening is "rocket blasting off," the proposition describing this what-is-happening, in reality, is more like a "propositional onion."

The external layer of the propositional-onion we could think of as "a rocket is blasting off." Imagine peeling this layer off the propositional-onion and we reveal "the

engines are blasting" and "the pilot is controlling" inner
layer onion propositions, and so on until we finally reach
the innermost layers of the onion with such what-is-
happenings as "bolt A12G is holding metal piece X42" and
other such minor details.

The point is that a single proposition such as "there is a
rocket blasting off" can be thought of as the what-is-
happening, or equivalently the purposive *ends;* yet this
outermost layer of the propositional-onion is not the
whole story. Concealed within this propositional-onion
are the means and ends (or equivalently what is called
here *how-it-is-happening* and *what-is-happening*
respectively) that taken together result in the
proposition "there is a rocket blasting off."

Again, changes in what-is-happening occur due to
alterations and differences in how-it-is-happening. Or
put another way, different ends may result from different
means.

Kant and the Noumenal Perspective

A problem was addressed by Kant regarding our ability to
experience a "thing-in-itself," or noumenon, characterized
as an object as it exists in reality outside of human
sense interpretation. The problem is essentially that we
have access only to our inner *ideas*. Kant basically said
that we cannot advance beyond the boundaries of our
sensations and thought structures, and hence we thus fail
to completely connect with noumena, or roughly the objects
and events occupying space. Our only recourse is to
experience phenomena, which is noumena after it has been
thoroughly processed by our minds. Actually directly
connecting with noumena is impossible according to Kant.
By definition we only experience phenomena.

We seem to quite easily translate our experiences of
phenomena into propositional structures. When a tree
falls in the forest, if I am standing beside it I
immediately realize that something-is-happening. The
phenomenon can be described with the succinct what-is-
happening phrase, "a tree is falling."

The problems start if there is no one there witnessing the
tree falling, which is obviously a very simple example of
some phenomenon. If I do not happen to be in the forest

58

the tree still will fall. However, since our ability to communicate is based upon our experience of phenomena, without someone's testimony based upon phenomena, we have no direct access to what-is-happenings.

If a tree falls in the forest and no one is there to witness it, it is not as if God creates a sign with the announcement "A TREE HAS FALLEN" and hangs it next to the fallen tree for our convenience. It would make the task of AI tractable if God did indeed trouble Himself to hang a cardboard sign, adequately labeled in English, next to all phenomena of interest for us. We can easily infer later that the tree has fallen, but that isn't exactly the point.

The problem is more like the way Kant put it, that we just have access to our own regulatory thought structures and phenomena. Everything physical that happens has to run through a gauntlet of perspective, sensation, perception, and reasoning processes before it registers as what-is-happening to someone, and then in order to communicate what-is-happening, it needs to be translated into a proposition or some other means of communication, such as gestures.

Let us assume, just for the sake of this framework, that if, for example, a tree does fall in the forest and no one is there to witness it, that there exists some unknown and permanently inaccessible "noumenal proposition" which describes this. Try to imagine that the proposition is always given in terms of some unknown omnipresent person, let's just say this "person" is God. As joked above it would be helpful if He created a cardboard sign describing each instance of what-is-happening to eliminate any uncertainty, and while this idea must have been rejected as a bit impractical, it is still helpful to imagine such a system of cardboard propositional signs created by God anyway.

In the Kantian spirit we can never truly access a so-called noumenal-proposition. Yet, we can still believe it is there anyway, inaccessible. The imaginary noumenal-proposition describes what-is-happening in the Cartesian realm of spatial extension, but it is a proposition "written" in a format forever inaccessible to us. For now it is sort of a placeholder.

The Importance of the Proposition

Why would the noumenal-proposition be important? Well, at least from the time of Aristotle the proposition has had a crucial role in knowledge, it is crucial in AI, logic, and communication.   When we refer beyond ourselves to external phenomena, however, propositions seem nowhere in sight; they seem to have disappeared. The fact is that you can't point at a proposition. If a tree falls you don't see a proposition written on a cardboard sign announcing the event. Propositions seem to come from within us, they seem to engulf and surround us, they describe our world, we transact in them, but even though propositions are often based upon physical occurrences external to our minds propositions don't seem to *exist* beyond our minds.

This is one of the huge problems in AI. How do we account for what is going on in the world if *we* have *ideas* and the *world* has *objects*?

If a tree falls in the forest and no one is there to witness it, a noumenal-proposition forever inaccessible to us can be *thought* to be created describing the tree falling. We can think of the noumenal-proposition as a means of formalizing what-is-happening in the realm of Cartesian spatial extension. This does not mean, of course, that the mind has direct contact with the noumenal-proposition, but it does mean, at least, that we acknowledge in the philosophical framework the existence of what-is-happening outside of the mind, that is, we acknowledge noumenal-propositions in the realm of objects in spatial extension. The framework upholds this relationship.

Term Clarification

Several coined terms were introduced in this section, so it would be wise to pause for a moment to further refine and clarify the terminology.

As a reminder in this section we are concerned not with mental occurrences, but with the physical, material, and generally observable aspects of reality in Descartes' realm of extension. As was mentioned above the usual approach in AI is to mimic elements of mental activity using material mechanisms, like a digital computer,

usually paying scant attention to how mind and matter
differ. Having dealt with mind in prior sections above,
in the extension sections we are concentrating on the
characteristics of physical, extensive reality.

The easiest way to envision the physical universe in
isolation without mental activity as we know it is to
simply imagine a universe with no thinking creature in it.
Now if there were no thinking creatures around, would
anything still happen, as characterized in our tree-
falling example above?

Let us assume that without thinking creatures the universe
would still operate essentially in the same way that we
now believe it operates. Of course, a proper empiricist
can refute that claim quickly, but it seems nevertheless
like a relatively safe, naively realistic presumption
needed if we are to advance very far. Thus in this
framework it is claimed that the world is essentially what
it appears to be with or without humans.

Although the preceding examples illustrated the terms in
use with reference to a thinking person, the terms in this
section were really crafted to be applicable without
reference to some person's perceptions. The problem, of
course, is that it is difficult to craft *anything* without
reference to some person's perceptions, so we have to
first visualize ourselves as the perceivers for basic
orientation of the problem, as we basically did above.

Now again at this point we are going to try to set aside
the experience of mental phenomena to the extent we can
and try to imagine the world without mind. In the first
place this is necessary because – in this era at least –
we can't place a mind in a machine. We have only material
components without mental characteristics. It's time to
sober up and get used to that problem, at least for the
time being. No more naive conflating of mind and matter.
Envisioning a universe with no minds gives kind of a blank
slate.

We can simply presume that the creator of the universe has
the rough equivalent of what we associate with an idea,
but instead of mental phenomena, as in the ideas we have,
God has something physically happening, that is a
something-is-happening as described above. Every
something-is-happening material occurrence could be thus
considered God's counterpart to the mental idea. The

structure can be seen to be similar, but the key
difference is, of course, that an idea is imagined to be
held by a human but a something-is-happening physical
occurrence is held rather by God (or the creator of the
universe or however else you want to phrase whatever great
power it is that is responsible for the universe – this is
not a religious point). Obviously too the physical
differs sharply from the mental – a tree falling and the
idea of a tree falling are much different things, in the
same fashion that my car keys and the thought of my car
keys are different things, as mentioned above.

An idea, to refresh the claims above, is an understood
proposition. The understanding of a singular idea
contains all the relevant beliefs which led to it, and
which also essentially delimit and support it, yet we
still don't really know how the process of understanding
works. We can cite the beliefs we have to support some
understood proposition, but that still doesn't quite yield
an explanation of the experience of actually understanding
an idea. An idea can undergo change, and thus reveal
different understood propositions as our attention and
experiences change. Propositions have the familiar
subject-predicate form.

A something-is-happening occurrence in the physical realm
of extension is akin to an idea in the mental realm. An
idea is a broad term which in various alterations yields
different propositions resulting from a varying mixture of
changing beliefs. In the same sense a something-is-
happening in the realm of extension can be seen to
encompass a multitude of interacting physical, material
components. Physical, material components support a
singular extensive something-is-happening in the same way
that beliefs support a singular mental idea. When focus
is shifted to some different aspect of a something-is-
happening physical event, a different noumenal-proposition
within a something-is-happening can be thought to be
understood by God. In the same way when we shift our
focal point within an idea we can realize a different
proposition.

A critical difference between these two classifications of
mind and extension is that material objects are physically
real and potentially shared by everyone when something-is-
happening, but beliefs supporting internal ideas are held
only by a single person. Thus the physical, extensive
realm of material occurrences – of *objects* – is rightly
the seat of all *object*ivity and ultimately truth. Having
a claim of $100 is one thing, yet having the reality of

$100 in hand (a comparison employed more than once by philosophers) to objectively show others quite a different thing.

Furthermore, a noumenal-proposition can fall under two headings: what-is-happening and how-it-is-happening as characterized above. In contrast, a mental proposition can fall under a multitude of headings, not enumerated here, such as commands, questions, desires, and so forth. To illustrate the issue a physical occurrence does not ask a question.

In addition, we are going to confine our analysis to the present tense only, thus at this point there is, for example, no something-will-happen or something-has-happened in the lexicon. Without human intervention and technology there only ever seems to be a "right now" in the physical, material universe as discussed above: there is only now-time.

Cause and effect are pervasive in both mind and matter, yet seem different in the different domains. It seems obvious that new mental propositions occur based upon logical manipulations of existing propositions, and in a way one proposition can be said to cause another. These sorts of mental computations are akin to that seen in common AI rule based inference engines. That sort of manipulation seems similar although different than physical events that chain together to produce some outcome, like opening a door and walking through it produces the outcome that a person has moved position – this could be viewed in our context herein as noumenal-propositions chained together in a cause and effect relationship resulting in new noumenal-propositions.

Summary

To summarize, if we have only a single object in our universe, nothing can be said to be happening. Interaction of physical components results in something-is-happening and if we wish we can ask "what is happening?" The answer to this question takes the form simply as a proposition, but the proposition has the true form more like a propositional-onion in which what-is-happening is supported by multiple inner layers that describe the means and ends to subsequent or outer layers. Changes in what-is-happening are due to changes in how-it-is-happening (the ends change due to changes in the means). We can characterize these propositions as an elaborate system of so-called noumenal-propositions which exist in some unknown form, independently and beyond the reach of direct access.

The form of a physical something-is-happening is like a mental idea – each associated with propositions. While an idea is understood by the bearer of the idea, a physical something-is-happening can be thought to be understood by the creator of the universe on the seemingly quite reasonable presumption that God holds a frame of reference and understands the nature of reality and thus *understands* a something-is-happening in the same sense that we *understand* our own ideas from our own frame of reference.

There is an unmistakable integration that accompanies an understanding – an understanding is a whole, not parts. It is easy to envision that if a tree falls in the forest, God understands the what-is-happening, that is the tree dying, and the how-it-is-happening which caused it, rotting wood. These are noumenal-propositions. A something-is-happening is a noumenal-proposition in the physical world understood by God. This is akin to the way in which an idea is a proposition in mind, understood by a self.

EXTENSION-HOW

This section of the philosophical matrix is intended to describe, within the context of Cartesian spatial extension, how things that happen happen. Usually when we talk about how things physically happen we concentrate upon issues like cause and effect, specifying the grounds necessary for something to happen. We usually refer to physics and mathematics. Since this is a philosophical framework intended as a basis for AI, however, we are going to try a more *meta*physical approach in characterizing certain issues of physical reality.

Something-Is-Happening Is the Result of Interacting Components

It seems that the chief result of interacting components in physical time and space is something-is-happening (using our most general term) as mentioned above. The

universe is full of a great many things happening
concurrently. We can visualize imaginary noumenal-
propositions existing basically in a realm of physical
objectivity, as suggested above, to describe a certain
something-is-happening.

Without individual physical components interacting in
time, either by some discrete interaction or by chemical
combination, nothing would happen. Uniform interaction of
physical components means that a something-is-happening is
a constant. For change there must be alterations in the
interaction of physical components.

Consider a mechanical wristwatch. Something-is-happening
is that the watch is a single mechanical device in a
certain configuration of interacting components.   That
doesn't describe much, however, just that something is
happening. It is not until noumenal-propositions
applicable to the something-is-happening are determined
that a structure becomes evident. "The watch's hand is
moving" then can be our uppermost noumenal-proposition,
here in the form of what-is-happening. Noumenal-
propositions could also describe how-it-is-happening.
How-it-is-happening is very generally that individual
components of the watch are interacting in time. Remember
that noumenal-propositions seem to be arranged in multiple
layers like an onion. There seems to be sort of a causal
structure in place – inner layers cause outer layers to
happen in a chain like an inference engine operating. One
gear may turn another, and so on.

The Independence of Means and Ends

The point to be made here, however, is that there seems to
be a kind of independence between what-is-happening, in
this example "the watch's hand is moving," and how it is
that this is happening, in this case interaction of the
watch's parts caused by daily winding. Alternately a
quartz watch operating with much different components
could be in consideration, yet the what-is-happening, "the
watch's hand is moving," is the same. Identical *ends* can
result from different *means*. In this sense the ends can
be considered independently from the means.

The same material what-is-happening, a result, can be
caused by different and possibly unknown interacting
components. Clearly this independence is an important
aspect of reality. It seems similar to the way in which

we understand ideas without knowing how we understand
them. The ends are distinct from the means.

The Physical Megafunction

If a something-is-happening is an operating windmill, the
noumenal-proposition, a what-is-happening, then will be
"windmill displacing water." Suppose we actually happen
to be building a windmill. We don't know *how*, as yet, but
a windmill could be built. If Cartesian extension, if you
will, makes a function call to "windmill displacing
water," the function that will return the result of
"windmill displacing water" must be such that each of the
necessary components are in place (sail, drive shaft,
trestle, etc.) and interacting appropriately. The result
is that the windmill is the effect based upon the causal
components interacting.

Although we may not have known at the outset how a
windmill works, we know a priori that a scheme akin to a
programmable function call is in place. We proceed by
calling another sort of megafunction (recall the
megafunction described in the MIND-HOW section above) with
the specific request for a function "windmill displacing
water." At length we discover that our windmill can be
built according to some mechanical specification, and thus
our megafunction essentially called a subfunction, which
we can think of as the how-it-is-happening of a windmill.
We had to make some sort of decision regarding which
function to call, in this case for a windmill.

The point here is that in physical reality we have a
function call structure readily in place: Whatever is
possible can theoretically be made to physically happen –
so long as the Cartesian-extension-megafunction is called
with arguments that don't violate the laws of physics.
This is the same sort of scheme and structure that we have
in thought. For example, if I wish to remember someone's
name I call my mental megafunction with the argument of
the person in question in a "remember-name" function
call.

A Something-Is-Happening Is Based Upon a Concretion

Thus far in this section we have discussed the notion that
the ends can be distinct from the means, and that
different means can lead to identical ends, as well as the

notion of the megafunction. These schemes taken together
give us a great deal of latitude in dealing with physical
reality. As long as we play by these rules it seems
anything can happen.

Yet, importantly, despite the onion analogy of discrete
propositions, the impression given us is firstly that a
physical whole is not simply the sum of its parts. In
other words a something-is-happening is not just the
chaining together of abstracted means and ends in the
manner in which an AI inference engine chains.

Any something-is-happening is firstly based upon some
physically existing thing, a concretion. Take, for
example, a something-is-happening of a freight train
rolling down the tracks. First we could say that the
engine is burning fuel. Burning fuel results in mechanics
that cause the train's wheels to turn. The turning wheels
force the train along the tracks. The tracks support the
weight of the train and guide its direction. Each of
those statements can be considered a noumenal-proposition
and it's easy to think in terms of chaining these together
to get the result of a train rolling down the tracks.

However, while this may seem to contradict what was said
above, when something-is-happening it is not based upon a
series of propositions. If only it were that simple!
When something-is-happening it is based upon firstly a
something concrete, existing, and happening in the
physical world - what is being here called extension.
The material world does not readily contain a group of
propositions, but rather that which such propositions
result from. The propositions are mere abstractions taken
from within the walls of concrete, whole, something-is-
happenings.

A critical part of the EXTENSION-HOW is then whatever
concrete physical occurrences lead to something-is-
happening.

Summary

In summary the *how* of extension generates the something-
is-happenings. There is a function call structure in
place akin to that of the mind via a megafunction which
specializes as necessary. EXTENSION-HOW can make anything

happen so long as the rules are followed. More than one component interacts in time to cause the something-is-happening to happen. We can usually understand how the interacting parts in material reality result in the something-is-happening by examination which reveals isolated propositions. While a something-is-happening can be understood based upon its abstracted propositions, it should always be borne in mind (however simplified this sounds) that the root of any something-is-happening is something concrete really happening and not the chaining together of abstracted propositions.

EXTENSION-TOOLBOX

This is the part of the matrix concerning the sciences which describe activity in Cartesian spatial extension – meaning the interactions of physical matter. Basically this is the realm of the traditional natural sciences, chiefly physics, chemistry, and materials science, as well as all the things capable of taking up space in the universe, and how things are in general put together (e.g., specifications for a windmill).

In constructing a windmill, for example, we would have to draw upon Newtonian physics, material science, and possibly elements of chemistry if we were to determine how some materials interact with the water over time. We would need physical materials as well as detailed specifications.

These sciences, like the sciences applicable to how the mind works, are not particularly integrated, although obviously there is a great deal of overlap. Metaphysics is rarely incorporated in traditional treatments of physics.

WHAT-HORIZONTAL

In this section we seek to make some collective observations about the categories MIND-WHAT and EXTENSION-WHAT in the philosophical matrix above.

For simplicity we can just refer to these areas (the MIND-WHAT and EXTENSION-WHAT depicted horizontally) of the

68

matrix collectively as the "what" or grandly as the "realm of the what."

In Both Mind and Extension the Propositional Form Is Apparent

A noumenal-proposition can denote either what-is-happening or how-it-is-happening. A proposition in the realm of mind we won't at this point further define and will assume for now that any legitimate proposition qualifies.

In the realm of mind, thought, which includes understood propositions, does not seem to occupy space. In the realm of Cartesian spatial extension, we have no direct access to propositions which represent objects and the interaction of objects – we have only the objects and events from which we derive propositions. As the propositional structure is of paramount importance in philosophy and AI, the term noumenal-proposition was coined. We can think of the noumenal-proposition as an objectively true physical and material proposition held apart from human interpretive bias. In mind we are dealing with the immaterial proposition.

We can consider the idea as the completed totality of a proposition in mind, and a something-is-happening as the completed totality of a noumenal-proposition in Cartesian extension.

An idea is presented to a *one* person, and we can readily imagine that a *one* God is the observer of physical, material events. A noumenal-proposition is then a basically imaginary proposition inaccessible to us, imagined to be from the viewpoint of an omnipresent God who is using a system of invisible cardboard signs containing propositions describing everything that is happening. We don't have direct access to noumenal-propositions, we have only access to our own ideas, some of which refer to something-is-happening.

For example, if I do see a tree in a park, I am assuming in this framework that the noumenal-proposition "a tree is in the park" exists. I am assuming that this is objectively true. There is no proposition at hand written on a cardboard sign which indicates that there is a tree in the park. Nevertheless, the truth of this situation is objectively and materially apparent. The noumenal-proposition is structured in the same scheme as the physical object under consideration: "a tree" is the subject predicated by "is in the park." Thus we are assuming that a noumenal-proposition is based upon the subject-predicate form.

Obviously, though, we experience a physical, material tree in a park, and not a noumenal-proposition that states the fact. I have in mind an idea which supports the proposition "a tree is in the park." My own mental proposition matches the noumenal-proposition.

A Single Integrated Totality

A critical point here is that there is, in both cases, a single, one integrated totality in the form of an understood idea or a something-is-happening presented to a one observer. I may happen to be looking at a tree in a park, but this seemingly discrete idea that I have still registers to me as integrated with a single totality of reality.

The last statement should, of course, conjure up images of much more than a single, barren proposition in isolation. We are going to imagine that God understands how noumenal-propositions fit into the totality of reality.

When we are talking about propositions always bear in mind that the proposition should invariably be considered in terms of how it fits into reality: the proposition is a mere focal point in an overall complete totality. It is how the proposition fits into a totality, or equivalently the proposition's focal point in a totality, that is the seat of understanding. If I happen to be thinking of a tree in the park, as above, my focal point within this total idea may shift to a park bench. In that case I don't really have an altogether new idea, just a mild alteration of the same idea within a totality.

Change

In general, how does an understood proposition – an idea – change? If I decide to alter an idea, I will a change be brought about. My will directs a call to the so-called megafunction described above. The megafunction, again, is just a catchall term to describe the generic process of

requesting change in a form analogous to a computer
function call. For example if I will to remember the
capital of Washington I issue a call to my megafunction
for that. The result is a change that alters my original
question idea into a total idea containing an answer. The
details of how the megafunction executed a get-memory sort
of request are in general not needed, wanted, or available
to me.

The Self, its Will, Good, and Purpose

We can associate the self and its will fairly easily
together. The choices made by the will constitute the
output of the self's mind. The input to the self, and
equivalently to the will, is also provided by the
megafunction, consisting of things like understood sense
impressions, recalled memories, computed numbers, and
importantly choices available.

Yet, any discussion of change should center around the
overall notion of purpose. We tend to associate or at
least presume a certain measure of good with each decision
(a point made by Aristotle) – thus with each output of
mind some good can generally be presumed as intended.
Obviously what is considered good varies from self to
self, and in some cases a self may have a perverted sense
of good. Granted that there are often conflicting
interests as well in the pursuit of good, but in general
it seems that each person is motivated to pursue his own
good. When we ask what the ultimate purpose of someone's
actions is, we tend to think that some good will result.

In the physical, material world our social institutions,
buildings, machines, and all other artifacts and
constructs are generally presumed to have some purposive
good. Even the briefest glance at the workings of nature
reveals purposes, but if we can't determine any purpose
for some mystery of the world, we tend to attribute it to
"God's will." Of course, the more science advances the
less we attribute to the Almighty. But God has always
been a ready default purposive driver to fall back on if
we couldn't really otherwise understand some mysterious
happening of nature.

Input, Output, and Function

The point at present, however, is how do we account for the interaction of those fundamental longstanding computer science notions of input, function, and output. How do we actually find these working in mind and matter?

The simplest way of looking at this is that constantly churning mental functions provide a single integrated input stream understood by the self. The self, the source of will, outputs decisions which result in more calls to mental functions (which we've designated as the megafunction to include all functions) and thus actions in the material world of extension.

So suppose you are driving along in your automobile and you see a stop sign. You understand the input to your self, prepared by your megafunction, in the form of an understood stop sign.   Your will, given this understood input, outputs a choice command to your megafunction (some mental facility) to hit the brakes. Some good has now resulted.

Machines - plainly in the physical realm - are generally easier to understand in terms of input, function, and output. For one thing we can simply examine machines directly. All machines were hopefully designed to be good for something.

Again, if we just don't understand some aspect of the world we tend to attribute its output - that is physical activity - to some hidden purpose of God. If it happens to be raining, it is not difficult to imagine that God has some purpose in this and that the physical raining is being input to a one God. Things that happen in the world, the totality of something-is-happenings, can be thought to be known to a one God in the same way that a totality of ideas are known to a one self.

Reasoning With Abstractions

It is unknown when some semblance of reasoning first made its appearance on Earth. It's difficult to imagine our predecessors as very intelligent, at any rate, without an advance to the stage of utilizing basic abstractions, hypothetical rules, and some chain of reasoning. We can

72

probably safely assume that these abilities, when applicable in any general, purposive circumstance, were the grounds for what we consider intelligence.

If our predecessors had been unable to form abstractions, it would have been impossible to identify fruit on the tree. Without the ability to form abstractions, the tree and its fruit would be experienced as the same thing, a whole with no parts. It's not really practical to pull the whole tree down and eat it. Intelligence based upon abstractions was vital to survival.

Without the ability to form hypothetical rules, it is hard to envision learning. It is probably safe to assume that modus ponens was an initial thought structure, running thus:

IF A THEN B,

GIVEN A

THEREFORE B

If a man-eating tiger is approaching then run. It happens that a man-eating tiger is approaching, so run. If there is nowhere to run then throw your spear at it. It happens that there is nowhere to run so throw your spear. If somebody is nearby scream for help. And so on.

Primitive man, outfitted with basic modus ponens facilities, could then survive and reproduce in all sorts of hypothetical circumstances. Throw in some basic Boolean logic (AND, OR, and NOT) and our primitive man forward chains his way around pretty well, hopefully applying his rules somewhat faster than an approaching man-eating tiger is running.

GOFAI and Chaining

"Good, old-fashioned AI," abbreviated GOFAI, is built upon this very structural foundation. We typically start with a set of hypothetical rules, historically thought out well in advance by an expert, applicable to some carefully defined and necessarily *narrow* application domain. Then by introducing facts from some problem immediately at hand an inference engine desirably reaches a determinate

conclusion by applying its rules. Bingo - artificial
intelligence.

But let us back up for a moment before considering AI
solved. Consider what the origins for this sort of mental
rule chaining may have been and whether this is as simple
as it appears.

If a primitive man is not thinking in harmony with events
in the world he is not going to survive. The structural
form of modus ponens, as well as its inferential chaining,
would have to originate therefore in practical, physical
occurrences.

It was claimed above that a noumenal-proposition, drawn
from the material, physical world, could be either what-
is-happening or how-it-is-happening. The what-is-
happening can be considered equivalently the ends or the
effects, and how-it-is-happening can be considered
equivalently the means or the cause. Of course, whether
something is a cause or effect, a means or an end, is
dependent upon perspective. The same thing can be both
cause and effect. The effect from one event, of course,
can be the cause of the next event.

The point here is that there was already a natural
chaining taking place in the physical world, prior to any
mind's rational chaining. The sunshine causes the effect
of the ice melting. The ice melting causes the effect of
the appearance of liquid. The effect of the ice now in
liquid form causes the stream to overflow.

At some point our ancestors picked up on this scheme of
events causing other events. They must have been able to
form cause and effect abstractions based upon varied
situations. Only outfitted with the ability to make
abstractions and a mind outfitted for the hypothetical
could they succeed in a general setting. There would have
been a certain unmistakable uniformity and repetition such
that the hypothetical rule structure became deeply
ingrained. The constant interaction with nature would
guarantee that.

The IF statement originated here deep in prehistory, long
before Aristotle's syllogism or Alan Turing's desultory
computer.

IF something then something.

The form of cause and effect, of abstractions, of rules applied to instances must have become implicit in all thinking, such thinking originating in and copying the form of observations of physically chaining what-is-happening and how-it-is-happening within a unified something-is-happening event.

Thinking Seems to Crush Rules Together

The problem is that, in general, the sort of crisp chaining that explicitly happens in GOFAI expert systems seems rather to happen in thought – to a great extent at least – in an instantaneous, subconscious, and integrated manner. And just because we can formalize a chain of reasoning in discrete steps does not mean thinking actually works exclusively this way.

Instead of a chain of reasoning it seems more like thought reasons by massing all of its learned rules and empirical data into a single, integrated, and constantly transforming concretion.

To illustrate this, suppose we took a chain of reasoning, imagined to be laid out in a horizontal chain thus: because of A then B, because of B then C, because of C then D, etc. We read that nicely left to right.

But instead of visualizing rule chaining in a left to right rule firing order, mentally stack the rules one *atop* the other. Then add to this stack all of those rules that you are hardly even conscious of, such as "if something had an end it had a beginning" or "two things are more than one thing." Then mash all the rules into one integrated "mega rule." Picture one of those junkyard car crushing machines squishing a car into a neat little block. Now we have crushed all of our rules into a single unit, an integrated mass. We are no longer able to clearly tell one constituent part from the other, our reasoning so interconnected and integrated that an attempt at finding a determinate form in the mega-rule is futile.

One Step Reasoning

What really happens when we are reasoning? In general, we usually face arbitrary, everyday problem situations by envisioning in kind of single step a desired goal or end state along with a general understanding of a potential resolution.

If, for example, my car will not start I immediately think first of purchasing a new battery. A GOFAI rule chaining expert system, on the other hand, would likely solve the problem by successively firing rules in sequence, collecting facts and firing rules as appropriate.

For example these rules might be tested and possibly fired: "If car not starting then check ignition, if warning light on then check alternator, if alternator light not on then on check the age of battery, if battery more than five years old then create fact record that battery is more than five years old," and onward it plods in this fashion. Eventually the system would arrive at a solution.

The key difference between my own thinking, having dealt with dead batteries before, and that of a typical rule chaining GOFAI system is that I simply hit on the most likely solution to the problem more or less instantly, understanding the problem and its solution as a single idea, not as discrete terms laid out in a chain of reasoning. It is only if I face some unknown circumstance that I become conscious at all of the details of my decision making.

Obviously the more I know about some problem domain the less time we spend consciously reasoning – a concept that employers are keenly aware of, not desiring to pay for an employee's training. Rather than chaining like a GOFAI expert system, it is much faster if we solve problems in a kind of holistic way in an area we are well experienced in. In this way we transition a single problem idea to a goal, only rarely pausing and examining our thoughts and actions if the situation demands a decision, for example if we have to gather information about some detail unknown to us.

Thus rather than the kind of neat rule chaining we see in the traditional expert system, typical human problem solving often simply leaps to conclusions, with the reasoner often scarcely aware of the logical steps along the way. What is more, we seem to easily leap to any spot in a chain of seemingly sequential reasoning, making alterations that propagate up to an overall idea without rethinking in sequence from the beginning. If we so desire we can demand from our mental megafunction an explanation, as for example how some part of our idea has come to be, and it will try to describe to us a path of reasoning from some arbitrary focal point to another focal point in an idea.

An Idea Is Not a Chain of Reasoning

And this is the importance of the *idea:* An idea is a single integrated totality, not a chain of reasoning, although clearly an idea may have a chain of reasoning embedded and hidden within it. An idea is both a single thing and a thing with parts: as an immaterial thing an idea is both and neither. We can easily leap from focal point to focal point within an idea, and when a focal point is established, that is, is the subject of our attention, it takes the form of an understood proposition; it is another idea, but yet an idea that includes the prior idea, thus not altogether new. Simply put, in reasoning we transition a single idea; we don't chain discrete and isolated terms.

Symbol Grounding and the Noumenal-Proposition

The source of what is known as "symbol grounding" in AI is in what is being called here the noumenal-proposition which really resides in the physical world. We notice what seems important in the physical world and generally hold the physical world as the source of all objectivity. As mentioned simply imagining one has $100 is not the same as physically having it in the hand. The material world thus is as close as we can get to objectivity.

The subject-predicate structure of the noumenal-proposition in the physical world is isomorphic to the subject-predicate structure of mental propositions. In the morning the sun physically and objectively rises in the realm of Cartesian spatial extension. Rising is physically predicated of the sun. Each time the sun comes up it strengthens the corresponding mental proposition in mind having the same subject-predicate structure.

We take what we learn from noumenal-propositions to envision hypothetical future scenarios. If we encounter some unusual outcome in experience that deviates markedly from our expected hypothetical scenario, we learn and revise our belief system – we alter our mental propositions and the ideas that emerge when we focus on them.

Thus we are in a constant cycle of checking our belief system – our stock of propositions within overall ideas – with the truth that we seem to find in objective reality.

Summary

This section described the realm of ideas as understood propositions, of a totality for one, of establishing attention upon singular focal points within overall changing ideas, of purpose and of good, of input, output, and calls to a megafunction that handles the details, of seeking goals, of explanation, learning, and modus ponens.

This is the realm of being embedded in the world, of being a user of the world, and of doing things. This is the realm of things happening, or simply *the realm-of-the-what.*

HOW-HORIZONTAL

In this section we seek to continue making collective observations of the philosophical matrix by grouping together the two categories MIND-HOW and EXTENSION-HOW. We can call this collective area simply the "how" or grandly "the realm of the how."

This framework makes the crisp qualitative distinction, again, between *what* is happening and *how* it is happening. *What* is happening involves a basically arbitrary focal point, a proposition, and it is brought into existence by means of the *how*. In general, this level, the so-called *how,* is characterized by accommodating *what* it is that can happen. The *what* is the result of the *how.*

The Versatile Megafunction

In general, at this level we examine the notion of the megafunction mentioned above. A physical variation of the megafunction drives how things are physically happening in the realm of Cartesian spatial extension. A mental variation of the megafunction drives how mental ideas are experienced.

The mental megafunction is commanded by a self using its will in pursuit of perceived good, but obviously a mind through action can cause changes in physical, material reality too. Thus, at this point we can talk about the mind causing external change – the mind can drive a unified physical and mental megafunction. The how then encompasses the entire notion of how things change physically and mentally. Concrete, integrated ideas in mind and concrete, integrated something-is-happenings in physical material reality are the result of the how.

Change Originates in the How

Commonsensically, alteration in what is happening usually comes from changes in how it is happening. We may will that some incomplete thought is made complete, for example, but nothing will change until we "change our mind," meaning that our understanding, provided for us by means mostly unknown to us, has been altered in some way. It is by "calls" to the so-called *how* megafunction that thought change takes place. In the realm of extension, a change in the way a machine functions can be brought about by changing one or more of its constituent parts, thus altering what the machine is doing by how the machine works.

The Megafunction Enforces the Rules of Reality

The megafunction seems to be able to determine possible from impossible "calls" to it. An impossible call to the megafunction is rejected. For example, if I said to myself, "remember what has already happened tomorrow" I am left with only the understanding that such a question is impossible. The megafunction rejects this at the outset. In the realm of extension, we cannot expect to drop a bowling ball and have it suspended in midair. The megafunction then seems to be fairly well constrained to operate within the walls of commonsense reality. If you "call" the physical megafunction by dropping a bowling ball it is going to head crashing to the floor.

The Question of the Origin of Propositions

The main questions to address at this juncture are:

How do we characterize how understood propositions in mind come to be?

How do we characterize how things that happen in reality come to be (or in the terminology of the framework, how noumenal-propositions, what-is-happening and how-it-is-happening come to be)?

Since at least the time of Aristotle we have commonly found some explanation to these questions using logic – be it term logic or newer, more sophisticated logics.

In the terminology herein, it was mentioned above that a single proposition is structured more like a gigantic onion (the so-called "propositional onion") than the innocent and simple subject-predicate, standalone construct it appears to be. Inner layers of the proposition at hand, the onion, can be thought to be grounds of the outer layer.

This analogy at least shows some of the intrinsic depth involved in the understanding of any arbitrary proposition. We are only seeing the outer layer of the onion, but all inner layers are needed to produce the outer layer.

For example, suppose, with an example taken from the realm of mind, that I happen to be thinking of a particular restaurant, let's say an Indian restaurant. My proposition would be "that Indian restaurant I like." Concealed beneath this simple statement are hidden layers of the "onion," such as the issue that I am thinking of, for example, a single restaurant, not multiple restaurants, that this restaurant will probably not have Chinese food, is not fast food, nor overly expensive, that this sort of restaurant may be better in the UK than in the US, the food may be spicy, and so on.

The simple thought "that Indian restaurant I like," the *what* proposition I am thinking, my focal point, is thus understood in terms of the totality of these other supporting factors, each which can be considered some inner layer of the "onion," and these inner layers taken as an interacting whole constitute to some extent *how* I understand my proposition. Note: I may not be fully aware of each of the constituent factors that led me to thinking of the Indian restaurant I like, such as that it is not Chinese food.

Change any one of these inner layers and the outermost layer will probably change. If the Indian restaurant actually happened to be a fast food restaurant, then that would change my understanding of "that Indian restaurant I like." If I remembered that the Indian restaurant was not open on Sundays, then it may not materially affect my understanding of "that Indian restaurant I like." I may like it even though it is closed on Sundays.

In the realm of extension, suppose I discover that my mechanical watch stopped. The so-called noumenal-proposition discussed above would be simply "this watch has stopped." However, we wish to change this to the noumenal-proposition "the watch is running." In other words we wish for our noumenal-proposition to alter. We desire to make a change in the realm of extension.

This change can simply be accomplished by winding the watch, and if we do that, and the watch is running, we have effectively altered *how* the watch is functioning. The "noumenal propositional onion" would contain many inner layers, each possibly representing some mechanism inside the watch, such as a gear that winds. We have changed the outermost layer of the noumenal onion by changing one of its inner layers, winding.

What has been discussed in this section so far concerns mostly what is commonly considered as the grounds or causes for something, be it leading to a change in a thought or something physically changing. As examples, the reasons which cause me to like a certain Indian restaurant are given, as well as the causes of a stopped watch starting. In both the realms of mind and extension

we can easily understand the cause and effect
relationship.

But even taking account of all the apparent factors in
some carefully constrained problem domain is just to
scratch the surface of how we understand things.

The Hidden Layer of the How

There appears to be what amounts to a very sophisticated
implicit framework concealed within the how. Just having
grounds, causes, rules, and results is not adequate. It
is if there is an *entire hidden level* that needs to be
accounted for.

When we start to address how something is what it is, we
must look beyond the apparent causes of it. We must even
look beyond the hidden causes. We have to look around,
behind, above, and below the causes, if you will. We are
aware of the causes of things because probably evolution
decided that was basically all we needed to function. But
*causes, factors, grounds, rules, laws, in short that which
makes up contemporary science,* are all formal abstractions
only seemingly separate. The problem is this: There is
nothing separate.

Returning to my simple proposition "that Indian restaurant
I like." We can, true, list those grounds which led me to
this conclusion. But what seems missing is what it is
that integrates each separate ground into the whole,
presented and understood by me as a single totality.

What leads me to understand some proposition, such as my
simple Indian restaurant proposition, is a raft of
supporting concepts, again none of which are in isolation.
What is referred to here are not just the sort of
categories found in typical ontologies, such as an Indian
restaurant is a type of restaurant, a restaurant has
tables and chairs, waiters, hosts, etc., and that sort of
issue. These are required, of course, but are not the
entire story.

We must delve down a level deeper. In this example, how
can a quantity of tables be considered as a single set of
tables in a restaurant? In similar fashion if we have a
quantity of three waiters are they then a single wait

82

staff? What does it mean that something commences, then
stops? How does a meal commence, then stop? How does a
restaurant commence, then stop? Because the waiter
unlocked the door? By opening hours? How does commencing
and stopping apply to thinking about this situation in
other ways? How do we know that if half of the tables are
empty a restaurant might be mediocre? If the restaurant
is painted, that means it changed. But what if it changed
its menu? How does changing one thing result in a
different determination than changing another thing?

It is realized that these are questions, not answers, but
it seems that all of these concepts are applicable at
once, and furthermore that they are all interrelated and
support one another, and that they each contribute to how
I think of the Indian restaurant I like.

The word "totality" keeps coming up for just this very
sort of reason. It's as if everything is used.

In the example drawn from the realm of extension, the
wrist watch that has stopped, we can consider this matter
strictly from the rules of physics and the interaction of
parts. These rules are formal abstractions. We have for
example rules drawn from the areas of materials and
physics.   But that still doesn't render an adequate
definition of how the watch starts running. Missing from
material science and physics is the issue of the simple
quality "not," that the watch is not running, but *can*
later be running. Where in textbook physics do we cover
the issue of "not presently but will be later." Now if
something is not, later it can be, *possibly*.

These are fundamental issues drawn from metaphysics, for
the most part completely ignored (rushed past would be a
better way to put it) because no one wants to concern
himself with anything that basic. But how can something
operating in the realm of extension be adequately defined
and understood if we don't even bother with "not"? True,
that can easily be programmed, but we that is not the
point. The point is that issues drawn from metaphysics
such as "is and is not" are integrated into the totality
of even this simple example, creating the how-it-is-
happening for the noumenal proposition of the watch having
stopped and then wound to start.

How the watch is working would seem to include other basic
issues like what its capabilities are, what it *is*. For

instance, it is a one watch, a single thing, yet made up
of multiple parts. If we take half the strap off, does
that make it into a different watch?

The How Generates Concretions

These difficulties are nothing new in AI. The point that
needs to be driven home here, at any rate, is this: Our
ideas as understood propositions are whole concretions, as
concrete and whole as anything in physical, extensive
reality. Indeed, the general megafunction (be it physical
or mental) seems to operate exclusively upon a basis of
holistic integration.

When I have an idea I do not have anything like a chain of
discrete terms and logic symbols. Quite to the contrary,
I have a single, integrated, understood idea. True, I can
focus my attention on some aspect of an idea, but I can
still retain the overall gist of an idea.

The *how* in reality, the versatile and general
megafunction, operates by generating concretions - either
ideas mentally or something-is-happenings physically. The
how surreptitiously slips into its creations all of those
constraints and regularities which saturate reality, and
which you aren't aware of, consciously at least - for
example that two is greater than one, that an end follows
a beginning, that a transition is a change, and all such
aspects of reality that metaphysicians have labored over
for ages.

Summary

In summary, how something happens seems to be based upon
various grounds and causes. The megafunction seems to use
these to constrain its results. It can determine the
possible from the impossible. Causes can be abstracted,
as they are in science, but we understand our own ideas by
integrating issues into a single totality presented to an
I. Even if we can specify all the causes for an idea or a
physical occurrence, there are still many factors which we
are not conscious, and these factors are primarily drawn
from the studies of metaphysics.

Reality never presents truly discrete terms. The true
mystery of the realm-of-the-how is how we can ever gain a

single understanding, an integrated concrete idea, from
what we typically regard as a mass of individual
propositions.

TOOLBOX-HORIZONTAL

Toolboxes in general constitute the "realm of science."
We can study and understand things from various
viewpoints, be it physics, psychology, philosophy,
electronics, robotics, neuroscience, materials science,
etc.   This is of course very useful, but it still
typically requires a human to interpret and apply the laws
to some problematic situation.

There is little yet in the realm-of-science, however,
which addresses typical difficulties outlined above, such
as the principles by which a megafunction could generate
anything like an understood, integrated idea from
seemingly discrete propositions.

FRAMEWORK – VERTICAL

Having summarized above the three major divisions within
the framework, the realm-of-the-what, the realm-of-the-
how, and the realm-of-science (toolbox), we will now
attempt to show how these distinct areas integrate, thus
forming our basic framework of reality.

The Absolute Joins Mind and Material Extension

To start we return to the realm-of-the-what.   This is
appropriate, since at this stage a prime consideration is
the basic working idea as an understood proposition.

Critics of the dualist approach taken thus far, of course,
will naturally be skeptical that the classifications above
will yield positive results.   The world, they argue, is
not mind and matter, but a single thing acting in a
unified manner.

It is more likely true that mind and matter are different
and are the same, thus they exhibit a certain likeness.

Philosophers since Descartes have had at their disposal a
certain bag of tricks to deal with the dualism problem.
The philosophies of Spinoza and Hegel, for example, both
essentially take the standpoint that both mind and matter
are subsumed within a single *absolute*. In the case of
Spinoza, mind is one attribute of the absolute and
material extension a second. Absolute is God in Spinoza's
system. For Hegel, essence is one piece and existence
another. In the Hegelian system (at least the objective
logic division) essence and existence seem to roughly
correspond to Spinoza's mind and matter attributes.

Basically both these philosophers found ways to account
for the division but integration of mind and matter,
claiming that mind and materially extensive reality were
not just simply separate and parallel, but are in fact
parts of the same thing: an absolute.

The details of exactly how the absolute combines mind and
matter are unfortunately somewhat sketchy. It is fair to
say that this is part of the ubiquitous problem with
metaphysics that has found its way into AI. If
metaphysics is ignored it becomes difficult to advance far
in strong AI, because strong AI is about everything which
metaphysics is the science *of*. Yet if metaphysics is
addressed, it seems like a waste of time, the questions
seeming too far out to apply. Thus a state of deadlock
generally results, with researchers often shrugging off
the problem and banking on the hope of "emergence" to
skirt around the whole problem of being metaphysical.

We Start With Everything: The Antithesis of Narrow AI

In answer to this dilemma, this framework tries to plant a
metaphysical flag, establish some foundation, and
designate a starting point: *everything*.

We take the relatively easy but uncomfortable conception
of an all-encompassing everything, mind and matter, for a
start. This should be held in contrast to the practice in
narrow AI of establishing a carefully constrained problem
domain. We are not going to first sit down and start
writing a program and hope later we can account for this
weird phenomenon of mind and matter working together, and
if we are lost hopefully we are no more lost than these

eminent philosophers. This seems like just about as
simple and general as it can get.

Therefore, the first major characterization in the
framework's integration then is that there is an absolute
which encompasses and pervades everything.

It seems to be the nature of reality to exhibit the same
patterns in case after case, and when we see something
that strikes us as new it is more a variation on what we
have seen before. In this framework, while each
categorical box has its own label, and is regarded as a
unique segment of reality, it has also been pointed out
how each box bears a certain likeness to others. For
example, *how* thought is created is similar to how material
things are created, as described above.

The *absolute* can be most readily characterized as
pervading everything, giving everything an unmistakable
integration, regularity, and similarity, thus being
everything. The absolute is thus implied within all the
categories in the philosophical matrix.

This seems to be the main idea behind the
characterizations made by philosophers of the absolute.

In the same vein the writings of Kant are helpful here as
well. While we cannot access what lies beyond our senses,
claimed Kant, there are certain principles, nevertheless,
that give structure both within and beyond the senses,
such as time and space.

We Abstract Something From the Everything

The important consideration next is that there is this
weird ability we have of considering some *particular*
aspect of the absolute (i.e., of and within everything)
while not losing contact with the notion of being part of
an absolute. I can, for example, consider the particular
aspect that today is Thursday but I do not at the same
time lose the idea that I am part of a whole, an
integrated reality of mind and matter.

The issue at hand then is: how does one characterize and
formalize abstracting something from everything?

As mentioned, in Spinoza's system a single instance of a mind would be a mode of the absolute's attribute mind. In the Hegelian system an instance of a mind and existence together, which roughly translates into a person in the *actual* world, is known as a "mode of the absolute."

In either case bear in mind that the important issue is that both mind and the material world operate under the auspices of the absolute, and that is how the gap between mind and material extension is bridged. Further, the absolute contains immaterial minds in the material world and it is impossible to conceive of the absolute without that relationship.

Now, normally an abstraction is thought to be roughly that which is held in isolation from the concrete. So perhaps we see a blue car, the entirety of which we consider the concrete. We want to tell someone what color it is, so we abstract its color from the whole car, the concrete, and say "the car is blue."

In this process we are in general taking some property that belongs to the concrete whole in question and considering it in isolation. The wheels really aren't relevant at this juncture, as neither is its fuel economy nor sound system. We are able to consider just its color apart from these other issues.

The Absolute-Abstraction

In this framework we will be taking some liberties with the standard accepted meaning of term abstraction. An "absolute abstraction" we shall define as any focal point within *the* whole, not just whatever the context happens to be. So returning to the example above, the proposition "the car is blue" is to be considered the focal point of our attention but is by no means the whole story. Also included in this absolute-abstraction is *everything else* whether applicable or not applicable, mental or spatial, anywhere in time, existent or non-existent, possible or impossible, actual or not, related or not related. There is *nothing in isolation,* there is no such thing as "the car is blue" without reference to everything else.

If we are going to abstract we must include not just what we happen to be referring to but we must also have some implicit means of placing the abstraction in its context of a single integrated totality, and this can be done by reference to an absolute, which we can consider in light of the philosophies of Spinoza and Hegel.

Now how do we tie all this together? As mentioned above, an absolute-abstraction appears innocently enough as a single proposition, but is also a focal point within and including everything, the latter taken to be equivalent to the absolutes roughly of both Spinoza and Hegel.

The easiest way of thinking about this is that an absolute-abstraction, while a proposition, is also a concretion. "The car is blue," a proposition, is understood as an abstraction, but the underlying idea which supports it, making it whole, is a concretion, an integrated single idea which includes such concepts as color, transportation, appropriate styling, age of the car, etc., all within a single absolute reality.

An Absolute-Abstraction Is Held by an I Embedded in the World

Just having an understood proposition is, however, only a part of the situation. There also must be an I which possesses the proposition to complete the form of the absolute-abstraction. An absolute-abstraction, then, is not just a single proposition considered in isolation, not mere terms arranged, but a focal point in the whole of reality, and what is more, a belief about reality held by an I.

The entire form of the absolute-abstraction is then "I think X" where X is any understood proposition that a person presently believes about the world.

X, the proposition, is input to an I, and the I can, in turn, output X.

The I is the source of will and desire for good, or equivalently what makes one generally feel better. The I is embedded in the world, willing and doing things. So when it is claimed that the "I outputs X" where X is a proposition, it could for example mean the self-willed absolute-abstraction "I think I will now have dinner."

The I has the power to ultimately direct thoughts and actions it entertains, which is the justification in the framework to say that the I "outputs" an understood proposition. We seem to exert control over what we say and do (except in the most extreme conditions) by calls to our megafunction which is in the realm-of-the-how. While the I thus outputs some X proposition, X is also concurrently input to I.

Again, we may understand that we don't understand some X proposition, which in itself is a kind of understanding.

Usually we don't trouble ourselves to think of the entire form, including "I think"; we are only aware of X, the understood proposition at hand.

To Summarize What We Have Thus Far:

1) A person is a mode-of-the-absolute, a term borrowed from Hegel. This means (in this framework) that there is an I, embedded in the material world, which is able to make abstractions from everything mind and material, collectively called the absolute, and we thus call these absolute-abstractions.

2) The full form of the absolute-abstraction is "I think X" where X is any understood proposition, a concretion taken from everything and understood as being a part of everything mind and material, a belief about some presently prevailing aspect of reality, and related directly to a one person, the I.

3) The I outputs an X proposition, the focal point, which is also concurrently input to the I. Input and output are now *united*.

The backbone of the realm-of-the-what is then the absolute-abstraction.

90

The Absolute-Abstraction is Supported by the Megafunction

Having now dealt with basic notion of the absolute-
abstraction, let's characterize how the absolute-
abstraction is being supported by the megafunction.

The megafunction, in general, creates an understood idea
in mind or a something-is-happening in material extension.
Implicit in this is the notion that the result is both an
abstraction *and* a concretion: For example, any understood
proposition is an abstraction, but the supporting
understanding itself is a concretion. What is more, the
megafunction in general works with both mind and matter
extended in space.

There seems to be a single, general, and variable X, or in
more common sense terms simply a single varying idea that
is always input to an I. This usage differs from the
everyday usage of the word "idea." Often we may say "I
have a different idea" and mean some notion quite
different than some present idea. But within the context
of this framework we simply assume that we have only one
variable, transforming X, ever.

The megafunction presents choices to an I. The I is the
seat of will and there always seems to be choices
available to it. The I outputs decisions. If I (here
meaning me) just noticed that it is sunny outside, my
absolute-abstraction would then be the proposition "it is
sunny outside" along with its understanding which *includes*
choices available to me. Perhaps I could continue
working, or perhaps I could walk outside. I understand I
have a choice.

When I make a choice my focal point in the totality of
everything, my single variable X, changes. The result is
that I often have a slightly different understanding of
the present situation. If again I have the absolute-
abstraction that "it is sunny outside," my understanding
includes the choices available to me, such as to "continue
working." When I decide to continue working, my focal
point shifts to the absolute-abstraction of "I will
continue working" which includes a new, slightly updated
understanding transformation of the same single X. The
new understanding includes choices of what to do next.

It may also be that some event outside of the control of
the I suddenly changes the circumstances. In this case,
the megafunction alters the absolute-abstraction, but
again, the understanding includes choices, some possibly
new.

Life seems to present the constant interplay and conflict
of the will and events. In general the I will pursue
whatever choices the megafunction produces that increase
pleasure or decrease pain. As we all know, however, a
seemingly minor turn of events even a little out of our
control can drastically alter our choices. The
megafunction, at any rate, seems to do a pretty good job
of constantly churning over the entire situation,
producing understandings of choices available, and if we
are rational we choose what is good, or equivalently what
increases pleasure and decreases pain. The wisest of us
choose the long term gains over the short term.

This life flow is the transformation of the single idea X,
a single mass, a concretion held by a mode-of-the-absolute
shifting in seemingly endless absolute-abstractions.

These transitions with their abstract-but-concrete form
should be viewed in sharp contrast to the more familiar
characterizations we have of automated logical reasoning –
there an assemblage of discrete terms in some kind of
reasoning engine, such as that which can be found in the
typical expert system, which at length produces a discrete
answer or reaches a goal. This drastic structural
difference is one of the fundamental problems in AI.

The megafunction uses beliefs to produce the understanding
of the absolute-abstraction as a focal point. Yet all
beliefs making up an absolute-abstraction are *also*
absolute-abstractions, yet are not the present focal point
in the totality nor do they generally present to the I
with a possible choice for decision.

Being Realistic: The Megafunction Handles the Relation of Inner to Outer

If what you are thinking, acting, and expecting conforms
to actual reality you are likely doing fine. Thus the
important relation within the absolute-abstraction is an
understood *mental proposition*, an idea, conforming well to

a *noumenal-proposition* within the scope of a something-is-happening. In this way mind and matter are related.

Problems really start in life when somebody is not being realistic, or in extreme cases has simply lost all touch with reality. A person that starts smoking at a young age but expects to have a long life is not in touch with reality. There needs to be a big picture conformance between the ideas and intentions that one has and the state of the real world external to the self. If there is too big a gulf in any of various ways between one and his world, problems abound. Holding the true for the false, the likely for the unlikely, the possible for the impossible, the realistic for the unrealistic are examples of inner ideas not conforming to outer realities.

An absolute-abstraction is by definition composed of both mind and matter. Thus, to the extent that mind and extension conform to one another realistically the more correct the absolute-abstraction can be said to be.

In order to reason realistically we have to associate the inner self correctly with the outer world. Stated in the terms of this framework, then, how do we associate understood inner mental propositions and an overall idea with outer something-is-happening occurrences which include noumenal-propositions? We are trying to align MIND-WHAT, MIND-HOW, EXTENSION-WHAT, and EXTENSION-HOW (along with their sciences) and show how these collectively lead to an understanding.

The answer lies in the overarching concept of the absolute which saturates reality and thus the framework. What the philosophers of old meant by the *absolute* was that the same *thing* could be found in different forms, that an essential structure pervades everything, mind and matter, and that is why the different boxes of the matrix herein are each variations of one another.

A thing and the thought about the thing may be different, but they may well share an *essential sameness*. When I see, for example, a happy group of people, it bears a certain unique essentiality which somehow leads to my understanding. I use the same essentiality later to associate to a different group of people.

Every belief has a certain intrinsic essentiality. Essentiality, it is claimed here, is not an assemblage of terms, but instead a single concretion. Thus essentiality is the backbone of understanding. If the megafunction doesn't have a unique essentiality at hand it creates a new one.

The Toolbox Provides Everyday Scientific Abstractions

The realm-of-science provides the working notions, universal rules, and laws that support the realm-of-the-how and in turn the realm-of-the-what.

Yet, while the sort of abstractions that science produces are generally useful, usually a knowledgeable person is required to supply an understanding of how a certain abstraction applies to some relevant instance. The problem in all seemingly simple problems, let alone tough, complicated real world problems, is how seemingly discrete masses of applicable propositions, instances, laws, etc., are combined into a concretion which can change and flow rapidly yielding abstraction after abstraction. There is no science, for example, which can combine the essentialities of all relevant beliefs into a single understood proposition, yet that is what seems to be required for strong AI. In general, science is better at describing pieces than describing wholes.

Change takes place slowly in the realm-of-science, and this realm may be incomplete and even inconsistent. Inconsistency and contention may result, for example, if one science overlaps another science's domain. Changes take place faster in the *how* and *what* realms, which makes sense because these realms contain particular, concrete instances which come into being and then pass away. In general the realm-of-science is of universals.

FRAMEWORK – HANDWAVING

Sometimes people explain their position while waving their hands wildly in the hopes of exhorting the listener into agreement. It seems handwaving compensates for missing or vague parts of an argument. Halftime sports commentators are some of the biggest handwavers around. Since no full blown strong AI theory yet has all the details, it is necessary to include a handwaving step to present the

raison d'être of the philosophical framework. Since this
is just a book, not a halftime presentation, picture
handwaving now.

Not the goal to Find Truth Outside AI

As a reminder, it is not the goal of the philosophical
framework to establish any philosophic "truth" of the sort
that can be used as a foundation for something outside of
AI, for example religion. It has been argued that one of
the tacit goals of traditional dualism was to separate the
soul from earthly existence, thus giving one a plausible
route into an afterlife without addressing troublesome
questions aroused by day to day science.[16] That sort of
argument is not the point here. We are seeking some means
of of representing reality in a new framework such that it
might make the task of strong AI possible.

This Is a Different Approach

Most AI approaches do not seem to work within a formalized
philosophical framework and usually assume the basic
tenets of the Church-Turing thesis: that if we can
formulate an algorithm of some process in reality it can
be implemented on a standard digital computer. Questions
such as whether some process is mind-dependent or based
upon some physical process usually are not included at the
outset.

It seems that the structure and act of thinking are not
really the same thing as a typical Turing state machine
and its progeny, as noted above. The most glaring
difference between thinking and standard, traditional
computing is that thinking, while certainly capable of
producing discrete ideas, nevertheless seems to operate
strictly inside a single integrated totality within which
abstractions are made. Typical, standard computing relies
on the processing of discrete terms which are connected
via explicit programming ultimately by some thinking
person. The framework is an attempt to classify reality
in some way that might expose these sorts of difficulties
before taking additional steps.

Aristotle famously said that a small error in the
beginning can lead to big problems in the end
(paraphrased).[17] If we design an AI system without
considering such basic problems as how mind fits into the

rest of reality, and other associated fundamental issues in metaphysics, we might be rushing past the most basic features of reality, not bothering to incorporate these into our design. The problem is that later on, deep in coding some new system, we are just left scratching our heads and wondering how we got that far, and what we are doing at all, and why nobody wanted to talk about metaphysics.

What is a self? Is a self single or multiple? Is a self not the same thing as an other? If something exists must it always appear? Can a potential occurrence be said to exist, even if it hasn't happened yet? How do we consider the interplay of quality and quantity? If a quantity changes how does that affect the quality?

Philosophers have addressed these difficulties at least since the time of the ancient Greeks, but scant attention is usually paid to these issues in computer science, usually because these themes are simply too difficult. It is far more realistic to craft very specific code that solves a specific problem within a carefully constrained domain using Turing computation. This is the form of AI we derisively call "narrow AI."

Thus we rush right past these deeper philosophical questions for the most part. After we have rushed past these basic metaphysical questions we are left with the basic and simple problem in AI of trying to write a program that can do everything. How does one write a program that can do everything if we have no philosophical backbone to build a system atop? It seems that such an approach is equivalent to starting at the end and proceeding to the beginning. Usually nobody wrote a section of code to handle something as basic as the difference between being and nothing, for example.

What is needed, on the contrary, seems to be some robust base and platform firmly rooted in a tough integrated ontology that takes advantage of those sorts of features of reality that are made clear to us on even the quickest examination. That something can become an other. That one can be split into many. That something may exist but not appear, and in some cases something may even appear that does not exist. That mind seems to be different in some critical ways from physical extension. That just having some fact written down on a piece of paper is not the same thing as its existence in space. That all these things can be applicable at once.

These are just a couple of issues, some examples drawn
from multitudes. The point is that it seems critical to
deal with these issues first, *at the outset*, rather than
rushing past them and hoping we can work it all out later
by some means of clever programming. We have centuries of
work available from philosophy to reference. Such work
needs to be incorporated in some starting base.

Final Handwaving to Conclude the Matrix

The Turing Test is said to be passed if an objective
interrogator cannot tell the difference between a human
being and a machine, each placed in separate rooms not
visible to the interrogator. Personally I *want* to tell
the difference between a human and a machine. That
doesn't strike me as the most important issue. The most
important issue is whether or not the machine can have
anything like the same overall *idea* that I have in any
arbitrary context. It is the goal of the philosophical
matrix to establish a structure patterned after the whole
of reality, and in so doing clarify the nature of the
idea.

Chapter 3: AI in the World – The Third to Mind and Matter

Introduction

Describing *how* artificial intelligence could work in the form of some design is no small undertaking. Accordingly, it is the goal of this chapter not to describe in detail a full blown solution to AI. Rather, we are going to examine in very general terms a means by which the above framework could be expanded to bear fruit in our quest for general intelligence. Within this expanded framework presented herein many variations of AI seem conceivable. Hence there is no single solution presented here but rather a general context within which we can work, that is, a general framework.

Spinoza Believed God Has Infinite Attributes

As mentioned above the framework bears certain similarities to the philosophy of Spinoza. Spinoza believed that there existed a single substance, God, of which an infinite number of attributes are possible. As it happens, however, only two attributes of the single substance God are applicable to us: mind and extension. Spinoza did not say what the other possible attributes of God could be - he only said that God has the ability to have as many attributes as He so desired, and what He desired were two attributes only.

In the spirit of Spinoza's philosophy we shall now expand our framework with an additional attribute: AI. This yields three columns: mind, extension, and AI. In the framework there are again three subcomponents to AI: AI-WHAT, AI-HOW, and AI-TOOLBOX.

Adding another attribute to God for the creation of AI may
sound a bit crazy, but perhaps not so much so as it
sounds. Philosophers have been in the habit of building
systems that justify, formalize, and harmonize with social
and religious goals since the beginnings of philosophy.
The philosophy of Descartes has been argued to have been
built partly for religious reasons (as mentioned above).
We have entered an age in which strong AI is sought and
many think it is possible, thus adapting these classic
types of philosophical systems for our purposes is as
justified as creating a philosophical system for religious
purposes or any other purpose. We need is a way of
visualizing how AI fits into the overall context of our
lives.

At the same time, if we do indeed succeed in building
highly intelligent, autonomous systems, who is to say that
reality does *not* conform to such an expanded Spinozian
philosophy? The truth, if any, is that every philosophy
has some primary tacit goal associated with it other than
"truth." Nietzsche had much to say about this, that is
the presumed drive to philosophic "truth."[18]

AI Is Not the Same as Mind Nor Matter

The first issue made apparent then if we accept this
strategy is that AI is not the same thing as mind. This
would seem to defeat the purpose on first consideration.
Yet, this would seem to clear the way at the outset for
those people who experience discomfort at the prospect of
a computer somehow being made equivalent to a mind. It is
made explicit here in the framework that a computer is not
the same as a mind. It will also please those whose goal
is not to find a way of duplicating human intelligence but
building other sorts of intelligence. As stated above it
seems that human intelligence is faulty anyway.
Improvements can be envisioned.

At the same time AI is not then considered to be part of
physical extension. Now we have a serious problem! If AI
is not be constituted of those things we have in apparent
physical reality, and is not equivalent to a mind, then
what might AI be? We have to imagine, as Spinoza did,
that other attributes of reality are possible. We just
don't know what these other attributes are.

The purpose of this framework is not the uncovering of the
"real truth" of reality, again, but some means of making

strong AI possible. We need some means of envisioning how
AI fits into our reality. If that means that we have to
pencil in some new attribute of God then so be it.

Thus we are imagining that God has made it possible to
create AI, but in the spirit of Spinoza's philosophy we
are going to have to *imagine* that there is an as yet
unknown attribute of reality that needs to be tapped. We
are searching for something, AI, and we have not found it
yet.

Add an AI Attribute Column to the Matrix

The main difference, again, between the intent of this
framework and Turing computation is as follows. The
Turing test is said to be successful if it can essentially
fool the interrogator into thinking that the computer is
an actual person. To succeed the Turing test the machine
need only appear to have intelligence. This goal leaves
one with a sort of incomplete feeling, because on the one
hand if the test were passed, yes, we would appear to have
artificial intelligence, but the problem is just as
stated, it only *appears* to have intelligence, and one
could reasonably worry that at any moment the machine
could cease appearing to have intelligence. The framework
described herein, on the other hand, puts the *idea* forth
as a first class feature as it is essentially the primary
component of the absolute-abstraction. If a computer
actually *has ideas* analogous to our own it would seem to
actually *be* intelligent, not just *appear to be*
intelligent. This is the hope, or course, and still
subject to a certain amount of hand-waving.

To be intelligent, then, a computer needs to have ideas
analogous to our own, but not necessarily identical to our
own. One of the interesting features of the framework
herein, as was mentioned in the discussion of the
absolute, is that we see certain similarities and
differences between the various categorical boxes in the
matrix. The issue of propositions, for example, seems to
prevail as a primary component of the *what,* for example,
in both mind and extension. The *what* seems to be
supported by concretions emanating from the *how*. We can
talk about psychology and physics in terms of their own
sciences. Each box bears a certain likeness to other
boxes, yet each box is also unique.

The strategy in creating a third column in the framework
is to base the third column largely on the other two
columns: thus in order to create AI we need to steal all
sorts of features from both mind and extension. That is
roughly what is happening now is AI research anyway; it is
just that this framework makes it explicit and puts to the
forefront and uppermost position the key issue of the idea
and the apparent interplay of mind and extension.

With this in mind, since we are creating an entirely new
column, AI, it is not expected that the propositions that
a computer holds will be the exactly same as our own,
although such propositions should be *essentially* the same.
Remember, each box in the framework is unique while
containing features seen in other boxes. It is not the
goal that an AI machine have ideas precisely equivalent to
our own. In the spirit of Spinoza, again, we are creating
a new attribute in reality, AI, which can be thought of as
being as different from mind as mind is from extension.

This framework differs from Spinoza's ontology, however.
The main issue to bear in mind at this juncture is that
the first row, the *what,* is the seat of propositions,
whether these are ideas that minds have or noumenal-
propositions which are known directly only by God. These
propositions are brought together by virtue of being
absolute-abstractions which are discrete propositions that
are a part of a totality. Such propositions are not just
terms, but a slice out of a totality which includes the
totality.

It is in this spirit that we need to think of AI: that AI
aspires to possess propositions which are part of a
totality – hence absolute-abstractions as described above.
However, a computer is not at all conscious in the sense
that conscious beings are, and this framework is not so
farfetched as to make a claim as wild as saying a computer
is going to be conscious in the same sense that we and
other animals are. However, given the nature of the
framework, it is not necessary that this be the case. A
chief characteristic of the framework is that likeness and
variation abound between its components.

So remember again that in the spirit of Spinoza the
intrinsic nature of the framework is such that we can add
new attributes, i.e., add new columns. After all, God has
an infinite number of attributes at his disposal. Why not
cash in on a new attribute of reality in the form of AI?
I make the grand claim of "new attribute" because in a

sense this is true: AI does not appear in nature, it is
man made, and if truly intelligent AI were to exist, AI
can be considered an entirely new attribute of reality.

MIND-WHAT	EXTENSION-WHAT	AI-WHAT
MIND-HOW	EXTENSION-HOW	AI-HOW
MIND-TOOLBOX	EXTENSION-TOOLBOX	AI-TOOLBOX

Figure 2. Now nine subdivisions or boxes representing three
attributes of reality.

AI-WHAT

We now add a new third column to the philosophical matrix
(Figure 2) and start with AI-WHAT. Our new AI-WHAT box
will be a great deal like the other boxes in the row,
MIND-WHAT and EXTENSION-WHAT, but new and different.

We already know at the outset that the framework is such
that each column bears certain likenesses and differences
to other columns, horizontally and vertically, as
mentioned. We can start our new AI column by just copying
the mind column wholesale over to the AI column.
Immediately we have to declare that, unlike mind, AI is
not going to be conscious in the sense that we are
conscious. That's OK. That doesn't negate the issue that
it can also possess propositions. The variability of the
framework allows us to make changes to neighboring
columns. Each box need only be similar to the other
boxes, not the same. In fact, each column should be
somewhat unique or there would be no point in having a
separate column.

General Characteristics Follow

The following characteristics should be thought of in a cumulative fashion, i.e., it is best to think of these characteristics by starting with the reasonably simple characteristics given first, and then adding the subsequent characteristics into the mix.

We Shall Start From a Phenomenal Perspective

At the start we are going to characterize the new AI attribute of reality in all respects in the way that it appears to us, *phenomenally*. In practical terms this approach at least gains a beachhead on the problem, as we can defer serious difficulties as to how it literally, completely works. This approach is inspired by Kant's phenomenal-first philosophy: We consider and understand things initially in terms of our experience of them but have no direct access beyond our senses to the noumenon.

The objection could naturally be raised at this point that if we are only going to look at AI from a phenomenal point of view, in other words, only from the way it *appears to us,* then are we not really taking the same route Turing did with the legendary Turing test? That is, if we only require that the AI appear to be a person, enough to fool an interrogator, while in fact not being a person but a machine, aren't we simply creating an illusion – a powerful illusion, but still an illusion?

Not necessarily. As claimed above in the handwaving section, a main consideration is that we plan for the AI to have *essentially* the same structure of ideas that we have, not just create such an appearance. That means, in the context of this framework, that a structure akin to that outlined in the full form of the absolute-abstraction must apply to the AI as it actually exists, in itself, not dependent upon any human phenomenal experience. We just don't know yet what its internal structure will be.

Is AI to Be Considered Mind or Part of Spatial Extension?

To start off, this new third attribute of the matrix can be considered in a sense similar to that which we think of modern AI programs such as *Watson* or *Deep Blue*. We get the impression when witnessing these programs working that they are intelligent, but we also know that they are not conscious of experience as we are, so they aren't properly mind as we typically regard it. Yet, when these programs (or in fact just about any program) are running it is frequently not simply acting like a typical material world automation, either, because it seems to make decisions and take initiative on it own, traits we ascribe to thinking. Thus an AI program often seems to be *more* than just a typical machine in the world. The result is that a program like *Watson* already seems to be somewhere between mind and matter.

That is the *phenomenal* impression we are left with – this modern artificial intelligence seems to be neither properly of mind nor mechanism in extension, but some hybrid that is neither. Perhaps that uncertainty is what troubles some people about AI.

If AI is not properly mind, not being conscious, nor does it seem solely part of physical extension because it appears to think, then what is it? We don't know yet. For the moment we only know it phenomenally as a new attribute or reality.

The Mode of the Absolute and the Nature of Input to Self

The reality that we experience seems to us to be a single thing – a single integrated totality as described in chapter two. No matter how detailed and seemingly discrete we can divide our objects and ideas – in short all that makes up our experience – these things are still part of a single thing: one seemingly infinite, interconnected totality. Change occurs within the totality, but the totality *itself* is unchanging and seemingly eternal.

This, one of the most basic and fundamental building blocks of reality, that reality is a single unified totality, has scarcely (if ever) been dealt with in the area of AI.

How could such an important consideration have been left out? As mentioned above, it was more important to rush past these difficult metaphysical questions in order to create a calculating machine, the computer. Besides, outside of a philosophy department, what scientist takes metaphysics seriously anyway? As long as we can formulate

an algorithm of our problem, isn't that all that is
required?

Or is it? Isn't it time for some backtracking? Even if
it is difficult? Why simply rush past a consideration as
basic as the integrated nature of reality? Shouldn't
Turing have made room for a consideration that weighty?

Let us say then that the primary characteristic of the new
attribute of reality, AI, is that it seems to us that it
understands that it is a one part of an entire single
reality - the very same single reality that we experience.

Again we are adopting the phenomenal viewpoint. We don't
yet know how AI is under the hood. We are only describing
how it could appear to us to be part of reality in
essentially but not exactly the same way we are - able to
form a distinction of a single self within an integrated
totality.

In order for the AI to understand that it is one part of
an entire single reality we again have to borrow from
Hegel, influenced by Spinoza and Leibniz. AI in this
context is a mode-of-the-absolute (as presented in chapter
two, a term borrowed from Hegel).

By this, again, we shall mean that the AI is inherently
within the single absolute. The absolute contains
everything. It is all that is spatial and mental, and
even whatever else there is. Basically the absolute *is*
the single integrated totality we are each part of, and
in, and as a mode-of-the-absolute a single AI would have
these essential characteristics, including the ability to
form understood abstractions within the totality.

Without being able to represent this fundamental
principle, that there is a single reality of which an
instance of AI is a part, it is difficult to imagine how
we can take a single step forward.

Not only is there only a single reality - a glaring
simplification in the structure of the universe - this
scheme also makes it convenient for each one person to
have only a single input containing everything
experienced.

We shall retain this feature from mind in the AI attribute. Regardless of whether we are speaking of sensory data, determinate thoughts and ideas, emotions, or what have you, there is never anything other than one massive input to one self from one reality.

There is a spectacular, simple beauty to this setup. Everyone gets one input from one one reality. Two persons would be entitled to two inputs, naturally, but still from a single reality. Of course now we are talking about AI, but the concept will be directly applicable. Each instance of our new AI attribute, that is each new mode-of-the-absolute, is to be considered as having only a single mega-input.

The objection can naturally be raised here that as humans we obviously have more than one "input." We have for example different sensory modes such as taste, smell, sight. That is true. Still, the point that is being made here is really the simplest take possible on this scheme. In AI the simple issues right along with the harder metaphysical concepts have been rushed past. While each of us does have more than one sensory mode, the fact is that at any instant in time we are experiencing only a single input stream *from which* we make distinctions, seemingly proceeding in stable now-time, as described above.

Like ourselves, we expect the AI to be able to distinguish between sense data originating outside of itself and its own internal ideas. In other words, the AI must appear to distinguish that part of its input stream originating from without from that originating within. Importantly, note the overlap between sensory data and ideas. Suppose we hear someone talking. The sound of the speaking voice is one thing; the ideas that we get from understanding the speech another thing. Yet, these coexist in the same overall conscious input stream. If one did not speak the language no sensible ideas at all would result.

Central to this notion is the basic idea that the single mega-input is directed to a single self. The question should arise as to how we shall consider the self in AI. As mentioned above, we can think of the self as the I of the full form of the mode-of-the-absolute, embedded in the totality of reality.

But there seems to be even more to it than that. The self or other I we seem to envision when experiencing the working of an AI program or really just about any program is equivalent the purposive goals of all people that developed it.

So, for example, what is the self that we think of as behind the scenes directing something as simple as an online banking system? We think of the entity of the bank and all the people involved in creating the programming along with their collective goal and purpose of profiting from financial trade.

AI Self - No Claim of Consciousness

Again, there is no wild claim in this book that a conscious AI is being envisioned. Still, we seem to attribute some sort of self to working programs, justified or not. I have often envisioned Bill Gates, for example, as the self behind the *Windows* operating system. There seems to be the phenomenon of a self attributed (rightly or not) to working programs.

What sort of self are we likely to envision from the AI described in this framework? It is expected that the phenomenon of self attributable to AI will be the collective impression that the AI produces in us, and these impressions will hopefully be of purposiveness, benevolence, and helpfulness. Of course, in order to bring these traits out the AI must have something essentially like a will. The claim can be made that will is closely associated with the idea of self, that will is essential for defining the self.

We can envision the AI, then, as operating in now-time, as having a single mega-input into a single self having a single will.

Transactions in Ideas, and Understanding Ideas With Beliefs

It is usually plain to us if someone else has the same or similar idea that we do. The new AI will be able to transact in the same general manner that we do - in ideas. Thus, the AI should be able to ultimately have the same idea that we can have in the sense that it has been defined in previous passages.

Everything said about an absolute-abstraction is applicable. We can think of an absolute-abstraction as firstly but superficially a proposition. Such a proposition is not isolated terms, however, but a focal point within a single totality, and presented in the mega-input stream. That is, an idea can only be considered valid if it is embedded in and related to the rest of the single reality, to something-is-happening.

At the outset the AI will only have a single main idea driving its activity. The main idea will be in a form of an assignment given by a human master. The critical issue is that what is willed by the I is intended as a means of completing its assignment, the single main idea.

As mentioned above, we seem to be able to understand ideas although we don't really know how we understand. We just understand. Even though we can cite grounds as to why we understand something, just knowing the grounds and causes of things is not the same as understanding.

An AI must have an understanding of its ideas. An idea is discrete-and-connected in the sense that the idea can broadly be rendered discrete in terms of a proposition, but the proposition alone is meaningless unless connected to the rest of reality.

An instance of AI can understand an idea based upon its beliefs. In this sense beliefs are many. The understanding of an idea of an airplane flying through the air is built atop beliefs of all sorts, such as those drawn from physics and metaphysics. That an airplane is a single thing, a one quantity. It is distinct from self. Interacting forces keep it in the air. Other beliefs could be based on rules derived from empirical facts, such as simple testimony of the senses.

Importantly, in a way all beliefs can seem to be activated in producing the understanding of any single idea. This is partly what drives the continual use of the word "totality." All basic beliefs drawn from a robust ontology, for example, regarding quantity and quality, could come into play for the AI simultaneously. That an airplane is a one thing, that if there are only two people

aboard its quality might be minimum occupants. A
syllogism that results in the conclusion that an airplane
is a form of transportation could come into play. These
are just a couple of many, many possible examples of
beliefs which we would perceive AI to have leading to a
determinate understanding of an idea such as this simple
airplane example. The understanding integrates beliefs.

The AI will gain an understanding of an idea by a call to
its megafunction. It is the single will – thought of as
one in the same with the self – which directs calls to
the single megafunction. It is the megafunction that
somehow merges all these seemingly discrete beliefs, such
as those drawn from metaphysics along with empirical sense
perception, into a single understanding of a single idea.

The understanding of an idea seems to be very roughly the
net of the beliefs that led to it, yet as mentioned the
understanding seems to be a different thing than the
fairly discrete beliefs that led to the understanding. In
other words, the understanding does not simply seem to be
the sum of the beliefs that led to it.

Again, what results is a single understanding of an
absolute-abstraction, an idea embedded in AI in reality.
In the same sense that we often do not know how we
understand ideas, an AI need not know what led to its
understanding of an absolute-abstraction. The realm-of-
the-what is the area of ideas, understood propositions,
noumenal-propositions and something-is-happenings. All of
these taken together result in the absolute-abstraction,
an understood proposition about some part of reality. The
actual generation of an understanding via the net of
beliefs is the job of the AI-HOW, essentially as it is for
minds.

In the interests of attempting to making the terminology
clear, let us firm up our definitions to this point and
attempt to summarize.

An absolute-abstraction is any determinate focal point in
a single totality (an absolute) rendered as an understood
proposition, present in the mega-input stream given to the
self/will of the AI. This ability for a one AI, an atomic
self and will, to form abstractions from a totality, which
encompasses basically all of what we are discussing
herein, renders the AI as a mode-of-the-absolute.

The absolute can be thought of essentially as everything involving mind, spatial extension, and whatever else there is. This means we think of the AI as inherently connected to everything there is by virtue of being a mode, or alternately put, an instance, of the absolute. It is within this absolute that the AI is able to form determinate abstractions.

With absolute-abstractions formed as understood propositions in this manner the AI gains entry into the realm-of-the-what, a kind of stock exchange of understood ideas and physical interactions.

We envision a single mega-input stream which is presented to the AI's single self. The mega-input stream includes what we traditionally associate with external sensory input, which is associated in the framework with noumenal-propositions, as well as internal mental propositions.

The essential conformance of the internal mental proposition to a perceived noumenal-proposition results in a belief about reality. The AI may regard something as true, likely, impossible, favorable, etc., by aligning its understood proposition, i.e., its concrete idea, with a what-is-happening or how-it-is-happening noumenal-proposition inside the walls of a something-is-happening concretion. The totality of *inner idea to outer something-is-happening* needs to conform *essentially* for a belief to be realistic. This is similar to the approach taken by Hegel.

A belief *supporting* the present focal point is itself an absolute-abstraction but doesn't presently serve as a focal point in the mega-input stream nor demand a choice by the I.

The mass of beliefs in the mega-input stream are coalesced and integrated, yielding a single understood proposition which is the focal point. The focal point is an absolute-abstraction presented to, yet nevertheless under the direction of, the atomic I.

We have identified a single main idea, the assignment the AI has been given as a transaction in the realm-of-the-what. The main idea will be that which the AI's will

seeks to realize, to fulfill. The will can alter its
focal point in the totality. Changing the focal point
changes the present absolute-abstraction, yet the present
absolute-abstraction is still connected to the main idea.

Everything is connected. When the focal point shifts the
megafunction is called. Calls to the megafunction may
return an understanding of the present absolute-
abstraction. The megafunction, again, utilizes multiple
beliefs which are themselves absolute-abstractions in
determining its understanding of each focal point.

Thus it is beliefs taken together which result in the AI's
understanding of a single absolute-abstraction, the focal
point in the totality. If the focal point shifts to a
supporting belief, that belief becomes the present focal
point, and importantly the new absolute-abstraction has a
different accompanying understanding, and has a unique
propositional form and a unique essence.

Beliefs seem to hold up ideas in the same way that bricks
and mortar result in a building. The building itself, if
thought of as an understood idea, does not seem to be the
same thing as the bricks and mortar, akin to discrete
beliefs, which constitute it. In other words in general
the understanding is of one single building – not just a
lot of bricks and mortar arranged in a pattern. Focus of
attention could shift to a single brick temporarily but
the understanding of the main idea of the building could
still be retained.

Now pretend that you are seated inside a brick and mortar
building alone. You have a single understanding. It is
the collective totality of the bricks and mortar which
lead to your understanding of the building. You have an
understanding of the building but you could still shift
the focal point of your attention to an individual brick.
But that only means that you are thinking of an individual
brick in the context of the building, you are not just
thinking of an individual brick apart in rigid isolation,
like a term in a proposition. It seems to be the nature
of the idea that we can shift our focus to those beliefs
which led us to understand it. We can see the bricks
holding the idea up.

Let's assume that each individual brick represents one
belief, but also assume that each brick represents some
different belief. The bricks are all related to one

another in the same sort of way that beliefs are related to one another. For instance, my belief that tomorrow is Tuesday seems to be related to my belief that yesterday was Sunday.

The entire single building is the result of all the bricks and mortar which constitute it. But we've now supposed that the bricks are each different from one another, yet still related in the same way that beliefs can be different but still related. In this analogy, the entire building represents a single understood idea. But if you shift attention to a different brick, each brick representing some different *belief*, there is a change in the understanding of the building, the idea, even though most of the other bricks have not changed. But do assume that the bricks are constantly changing, at the same rate that we learn and acquire sense data. Thus the building itself – the understood idea – is constantly changing.

It does seem strange to think that the AI could have at each instant a *single changing understood idea*, but that is the intent here. The single understood idea corresponds to the building changing in relation to its changing bricks. We can think of the mortar as akin to that which ties bricks – beliefs – in relation to one another. In this analogy you would be sitting inside the building experiencing the building change. You have a now-time clock mounted on the wall of the building which allows you to determine how time relates to the changing building surrounding you. The net of everything which the building presents to you is akin to the mega-input stream. The single understanding of the bricks – the beliefs – is given to you by the megafunction, but you don't know how or from where the mega-function works. Indeed you don't care. You, the bricks and mortar, and the building as a whole can be thought of as akin to the mode-of-the-absolute.

Summary of General Characteristics

In summary, we can envision that the AI holds at all times a single absolute-abstraction. A single mega-input stream is generated by a single megafunction input to one single AI self with one will. The mega-input stream is a totality of changing beliefs about reality with a focal point of an understood proposition. The focal point may include alternatives available for selection. The self/will, or the I, can output choices. This entirety can be taken as a single mode-of-the-absolute.

What it Does

The intention, again, is that the AI accept an assignment
in the form of a *main idea* from a human master, gain
adequate understanding of this idea, and carry out the
assignment specified in the main idea.

Now, it was ventured above that there is only a single
varying absolute-abstraction based upon an entirety of
beliefs. The main idea, the assignment given to the AI,
is the focal point of the varying absolute-abstraction at
the outset.

The role of AI is strictly in servitude to a human master.
All communication between human and AI is transacted in
ideas. The main idea, which starts the process, describes
a present situation along with a desired end to the
situation, i.e., the goal and purpose of the assignment is
specified at the beginning. The AI attempts to transform
the main idea so that its desired end, its goal, is
objectively realized. This transformation is done in now-
time.

A chief characteristic of the main idea given by the human
master to the AI is that this main idea contains both the
potential desired end or outcome *and* the present state of
affairs as far as can be ascertained as an understood
concretion. The nature of the idea as it has been
expounded here is not a state-first nature. We say only
that an idea is in a potentially transforming now-state.
If necessary the focal point can shift to an underlying
belief that is more state-centric.

At first it will seem a little awkward to get used to this
approach; this is a philosophy intended to more closely
resemble the way we think. In computer science, on the
other hand, we could easily have, for example, one field
initially set to a start state and later changed to a
discrete goal state. Next we issue a "run" command and
the computer searches for a means of getting from start to
goal.

Fine – but here we must start thinking such that our rough
equivalent of a single field is *both* the start and goal
state. Moreover, that our single field, while discrete,

is at the same time nevertheless intrinsically connected
to a goal state and all the intermediate search terms and
everything else in an equivalent program, the entire thing
a transforming understood concretion. This single
combined start and goal state is simply in now-state
containing some of the past and some of the future.

That paradigm seems to be the message that reality is
sending to us, not just in the massive level of
interconnections seen in the brain and the way we think,
but also in the manner in which physical reality appears.
An open door could be closed later. Those are not two
separate states but a single, concrete, and understood
belief in the realm-of-the-what. Thus we consider start
state and goal state to be effectively embedded in the
main idea.

The task is to transform this main idea such that its
desired end is objectively realized. The question is then
what we mean by "objectivity realized."

Typically we think of objectivity as a means of
characterizing some object of our attention in the
external world completely without respect to any
individual's particular mental perceptions and
interpretations. By subjective we mean, of course, the
opposite – a subjective judgment is a more or less
personal viewpoint. It is not always clear what is
subjective and what is objective, but for the moment just
keep the basic idea in mind.

In the context of this framework it will be the case that
the AI will maintain an extensive set of beliefs. These
beliefs will *each* contain both a subjective, inner aspect
and objective, outer derived aspect. It is how these
aspects combine in beliefs that is the issue.

To the extent that the subjective part of the belief
conforms to its objective part the more aligned the belief
is with reality, the more correct or plausible the belief.
If I think today is Tuesday but the calendar says it is
Friday my belief is not well aligned with reality. A 90
year old man who thinks 18 year old girls are generally
going to be attracted to him is not quite in touch with
reality.

We will assume for the moment that the AI has gained an understanding of its main idea assignment. The AI's will is such that it will continue to work on its assignment until it understands that the desired end has been realized. Any time the desired end has not been realized, or in other words reality doesn't conform to the main idea, in general the AI will call its megafunction, which will likely return some options for proceeding.

Now, let us assume that our AI is embedded in a robot. We give the robot the main idea assignment of picking up an object.

Given an understanding of this simple assignment, the robot's self/will calls its megafunction because the desired end has not been realized. The megafunction analyzes its beliefs about the location of object, its beliefs about the robot's arms, and some or all the rest of its beliefs drawn from physics, metaphysics, and whatever else is appropriate and returns to the robot's self/will (or simply the I) a recommendation to grasp the object with its right robotic arm. The robot's self/will decides to pick up the object with its right robotic arm. To do this, the robot's self/will calls the megafunction with the command to pick up the object with its right robotic arm. The megafunction activates the right arm and the object is picked up. As the object is being picked up, the mega-input stream is changing, and thus the beliefs held by the AI are changing.

The megafunction essentially uses the totality of the AI's beliefs to generate the mega-input stream. The robot's understanding of the entire situation and overall idea are kept up to date in now-time by the megafunction. If something is not understood the megafunction returns an understanding that it does not understand. And again, there is just a single now-state.

There Are Essentially Three Main Aspects to the Robot Example Above

The **first** is that we can visualize the self/will of the AI in the robot as being atomic. The self is one and the same as the will, indivisible and constant. Further, this atomic self/will is similar to Turing's oracle, in that it can make a decision in a single operation. The self/will can override what the megafunction recommends. The buck stops with the self/will. In addition to this, the self/will is the target of the mega-input stream and the choices of the self/will constitute the output of the AI.

Naturally when we talk about what something does in technology we think in terms of input, function, and output - but only output really does anything. For example, in Turing computation we may alter the logical tape. Programs display data and robots move things. An AI purely self contained with no noticeable effect in the real world would be disappointment indeed, no matter how clever! The most impressive reasoning facility possible that did nothing noticeable would be as worthless as a genius who conjured up the most amazing inventions but never told a soul.

At this juncture, however, keep in mind that we are discussing AI that is akin, although not the same as, a mind. When humans perform some willful action the origin of the action is from within - from the self. We attribute other people's actions to the choices they make. Yet when we decide to speak, when we will ourselves to speak, we really don't know how we speak, we just speak. When we move our arm, we only think to move it and it moves. How we actually move it is something we need not be aware of. Indeed, being aware of the details of moving an arm, such as a command to move a specific tendon by firing a specific set of neurons, would be far more detail than we could hope to handle.

With this in mind, output in this framework, in the first place, is simply choices made by the self/will. It is one of the jobs of the megafunction to present choices to the self/will, then attempt to implement whatever the self/will selects. A simple example of a choice presented by the megafunction to the self/will would be the selection of the next focal point, the next absolute abstraction.

The first way we visualize this is in the action the robot takes in our example to reach for the object. It must make a choice for arm movement, and when it does its arm moves. We can think of the choice and the movement collectively as output. When the arm is moved the AI's beliefs about the external world change. The megafunction updates its beliefs according to output actions.

At this point in the framework we are not going beyond discussing changes to the AI's belief systems when output is realized. Obviously, some choice made by a robot to move an arm must be accompanied by the action of movement. However, within this section we are simply going to stop at the belief stage and not trouble ourselves yet as to how, for example, a robot actuator is physically to be operated. Thus, in the context of our example, if the robot chooses to move its arm, the megafunction is called to move the arm. We will assume that the megafunction has the means to physically command the movement of the robotic arm. The megafunction will change the belief that the robot has about the location of its arm when it moves it.

The critical issue is that we need to be aware that any output is associated with a change in a belief and by that stroke with the mega-input stream. From our own standpoint, as human beings, all we really have present to mind when we move an arm is the belief that we move our arm. It is at this level that we are interested in at this juncture.

Notice, however, that we have defined output to be associated with choices made. A choice could be for some wholly internal action, however. Suppose someone tells the AI to remember the name of the mayor of Seattle. When the AI chooses to remember the name of the mayor, we can consider that to be willful learning which can later be demonstrated.

This scheme makes it a little easier to interact with the AI. We may give an assignment to our AI not to perform some physical action, but to learn something, or remember something. In this case we can associate such learning or remembering with the AI's output. We want the AI to perform some *action*. This will occur to us in a form starting with a verb, such as "move that object, remember that sequence, take out the trash," and the like. The AI must *choose* to perform some verb. Thus the AI's output is essentially whatever it does for us resulting from the choices its self/will makes.

Importantly, whenever a belief is changed, even a belief based upon an output, the mega-input stream changes, since as discussed the totality of beliefs constitute the understanding that the megafunction generates in the mega-input stream. When the robot in our example chooses to move its arm, this action is considered to be an output in this framework. The belief held by the robot about what its right arm is doing changes. This changed belief about

its right arm is taken up in the mega-input stream along
with all other beliefs.

Thus any output is immediately also an input to self/will.
This of course brings up the important notion of feedback.
We can envision the mode-of-the-absolute as saturated in
feedback and analog in nature. A movement of a robotic
arm is instantly transformed into linked beliefs regarding
not only the robot's arm and the object, but also beliefs
related to physics and metaphysics.

For instance, in metaphysics the belief would exist that
the object is not the same as the robot's arm. These are
two separate things. Two is a belief about quantity. The
action of movement would naturally have a beginning and
end - these beliefs again are drawn from metaphysics.
Movement of the arm utilizes beliefs about time and space,
and these are drawn from physics.

The self/will is expected to make good choices. We define
a good choice as one which helps in the transformation of
the desired end into the realized end within the main
(i.e., assigned) idea. The AI will associate the good
with the realization of its desired end. Conversely,
whatever it is that inhibits the realization of the
desired end is generally bad.

When the self/will makes a choice, the focal point of the
main idea changes to its choice. Yet, a subsequent change
in the totality of beliefs can lead to a new understanding
of the situation at hand. When this happens a new choice
must be made, beliefs again change, and the process
continues with another choice made by the self/will and a
new focal point in the totality. This cycles until the
understanding reports that the desired end of the main
idea has been objectively realized. Importantly the main
idea does not in any way disappear if the focal point
changes; the main idea is transformed. This is akin to
the way that humans can work toward a main goal while
diverting attention to minor but relevant details.

If the desired end of the main idea is objectively
realized, the AI can report to the human master that the
assignment has been completed.

It may be that there is some interruption that results in
a belief being introduced such that the understanding

deems it is important to notify the self/will and ask it
to choose a course of action. When this happens the
focal point changes in the main idea in an unexpected
manner. Suppose you are busy with some task and your
smartphone rings. Your attention is drawn to the ringing,
but you immediately ignore it and go back to your task.
This may also happen in the realm of AI. There may be a
sudden interruption which changes the focal point
momentarily. The self/will elects to ignore the change in
focal point. The original focal point persists.

Note that the focal point is the same as the choice point.

The mega-input stream is the **second** important aspect in
our example above. Input to the AI's self/will chiefly
includes an understood proposition as the focal point,
however this is a concretion composed of nothing short of
the totality of beliefs (some derived from external sense
activity), understandings, and choices available. A
belief could be, for example, a memory, or something in
the present, like the object in front of the robot. Other
examples would be beliefs about time and space.

The nature of external sensory input to the AI is confused
since within this framework the AI's input is not to be
considered in the manner which is typical for computer
input, as for example an input raw data string of bits in
packets of the sort we might encounter in everyday
processing.

Input of external sense data within this framework follows
somewhat of a Kantian stance. Kant said that we cannot
establish a direct connection to noumena. We have only
phenomena under Kant's system. Hence, akin to this, when
external raw sensor data reaches the self/will in the
mega-input stream it is already in some form akin to an
understood mental proposition, representing in general the
objective side of the absolute-abstraction.

What is happening externally to the AI is the driving
force of objectivity. The AI is not intended to be an
isolated "brain in a vat," like that depicted in *Spock's
Brain,* a *Star Trek* episode: Mr. Spock's brain has been
totally removed, placed in a stationary container, and is
being used to control an alien facility without Mr. Spock
knowing what is going on. Since we are devising a
framework for AI embedded in the world, on the other hand,

it is necessary that immediate phenomena derived by the
sensors have an intrinsic, objective part in beliefs.

This framework upholds the notion that, in general, an
externally existing noumenal-proposition is to be aligned
essentially with an inner proposition, and it is only if
an external overall something-is-happening conforms well
to an internal idea in its totality that a *belief is
realistic*. The absolute-abstraction of the AI, in other
words, has some firm connection with what resides outside
of itself.

The basic unit of representation in this framework, again,
is the belief. When all beliefs are taken as an
integrated totality with a focal point the result is the
AI's overall understanding of an absolute-abstraction.
This is what should in general appear in the mega-input
stream to the self/will.

The **third** issue is the megafunction, already discussed
above. Its chief job is to provide the self/will with an
understanding by generating the mega-input stream.

It is the megafunction which provides understanding,
accumulating beliefs into an abstract concretion, but it
is the self/will that understands. It is not necessary
for the self/will to know how it understands, only that it
understands. The megafunction creates the understanding
based upon its totality of beliefs, each having to various
degrees external sense origins and roots in reasoning.

One of the ways of providing an understanding is by
presenting choice options to the self/will. In our
example above, the main idea specifies that an object is
to be picked up. But suppose our robot has two arms. The
desired end of the main idea is that the object be picked
up, but it does not matter which arm is used for picking
up. Perhaps one arm is closer to the object than the
other. The megafunction conveys an understanding to the
self/will that it has a choice, and that the recommended
option is for the closest arm to do the pickup.

It may be the case that the understanding, again based
upon the present totality of beliefs, determines that more
reasoning is required. Suppose that in fact the object
the robot has been ordered to pick up has a second object
placed atop it. The understanding initially determines

that two choices can be made. Either it can grab the
object and risk breaking the object atop it, or engage in
further reasoning, producing additional choices. If the
uppermost object happened to be an expensive piece of
electronics as opposed to a child's toy gadget it would
make a significant difference. It may be that it is
necessary to pick up the object and make this sort of
determination.

This is a very simple case, of course, but it indicates
the choices that must be made, and choices are not just in
a physical action form, but also in the form that we
usually associate with mental operations, that is a choice
to defer physical action and pursue further reasoning and
deliberation.

Remember that one of the global issues in this framework
is that while we see similarities between the various
categories and boxes, nevertheless there are always
differences too. The understanding generated by the
megafunction should not be thought of as identical to the
understanding we experience. It is enough that the AI
captures the *essence* of understanding only, not that its
understanding is identical in structure to our own.
Indeed, as a reminder it is not the point of this
framework to find a way to duplicate human thinking.

The Issue of Change Is Important

How does anything change in the AI? In general, change
can be initiated in at least two main ways. One source of
change is due to the self/will making choices that the
understanding presents to it. A robot may have the option
of lifting one arm or the other. Changes due to varying
external phenomena will also result in change. If an
object is moved the AI's understanding of the situation
changes accordingly. Change means changes anywhere in the
entire system of beliefs leading to changes in overall
understanding. Of course the self/will could make a
choice at precisely the same instant as some external
phenomenon changes. In this case changes throughout the
belief system and thus the overall understanding are
concurrent. Again, we think of the AI as having a single
understanding of an overall absolute-abstraction based
upon its totality of beliefs, each containing both inner
and outer content.

Summary

In summary, then, we envision the AI as a mode-of-the-absolute, a term borrowed from Hegel, here meaning that the AI has an understanding and a representation of its place in the totality of a single integrated reality by virtue of possessing a single understood absolute-abstraction which varies based upon its entire spectrum of beliefs. All beliefs must conform the inner, mental to the outer, noumenal, thus beliefs must have a subjective as well as objective basis. The AI's task is to accept a main idea from a human master in the form of an assignment having a desired end. The AI's self/will must make choices, its good choices, that transform the main idea, leading ultimately to the objective realization of its desired ends.

AI-HOW

Introduction

It is the job of the AI-HOW to generate a mode-of-the-absolute, as characterized above.

The AI-HOW can also be thought of as very roughly akin to a typical AI inference engine, at least in the sense that it is trying to solve some problem, but instead of common forward or backward chaining search, usually advancing from discrete start to goal state, we are instead going to be concerned with transforming a single integrated absolute-abstraction, always in a now-state, to a desired end. The now-state contains implicit beliefs about past and upcoming, expected events. The transformation of the single main idea, inherently containing both start and goal states, is complete when the AI's assigned desired ends become objectively realized ends.

The question should naturally arise now regarding what exactly it is that the AI-HOW is supposed to be generating. That is, what is meant by "generating a mode of the absolute" and generating an idea, and all similar questions?

122

Again, we have recourse to thinking of the AI phenomenally, in the way that it appears to us. We can think, firstly, of the AI-HOW as generating a thing, an instance, a mode-of-the-absolute, which as philosophized above is in the AI column neither part of physical extension nor mind, but is to be considered a new attribute of reality, certainly not human, but nevertheless of the general form "I think X," in which both "I think" and X are part of a single understood idea, an absolute-abstraction.

Remember, again, that we are using philosophy as a tool, not in service to religious, political, aesthetic, nor moral ends, not in search of absolute truths, but as a means of attempting to make strong AI possible. We are envisioning *what* AI would seem to potentially be doing, and from that *how* it could do *what* it could do. We are not proceeding from a Turing machine to a proposed AI; we are using analogies from reality to uncover how general AI might work.

This strategy makes deliberate use of an analogy to Spinoza's contention that reality consists of a single substance, God, an absolute, who has the ability to have an infinite number of attributes. We are proceeding on the assumption that we can introduce a new attribute to reality, characterized by the AI-WHAT, AI-HOW, and AI-TOOLBOX, conforming to the classifications and essentialities we have made for physical extension and mind in the philosophical matrix above.

Bearing this in mind, in the same way that the AI-WHAT was like the categories of MIND-WHAT and EXTENSION-WHAT, the AI-HOW should be like MIND-HOW and EXTENSION-HOW within the realm-of-the-how.

As explored above, the *how* seems to chiefly concern itself with interacting components in time – how an automobile works in extension can be seen in the interaction of its gears, wheels, and so forth, and how a mind works in the interaction of its constituent functions, such as the ability to understand syllogisms, learn, form memories, all of which contribute to a constellation of beliefs which are used to form concrete understandings.

We are going to keep thinking phenomenally here, again, in the AI-HOW section. The bottom line is that we are going to consider solutions which are presently impossible, yet even so fall under the known categories in the philosophical matrix above. We are going to determine how AI works initially starting from how it might appear to us.

We are going to visualize phenomenally then how three main interacting components below, the megafunction, oracle, and pineal connector could collectively produce AI. This is without defining how AI really works, as a thing-in-itself.

It will be necessary, however, to eventually introduce new methods which as yet cannot be said to exist. Remember that we have an entirely new attribute of reality, that while it shares the same classification (namely the WHAT/HOW/TOOLBOX form) with mind and extension, will nevertheless be different in its own right, in the same way that mind is different from extension (as noted above). It will presumably be up to us to discover these new methods in due course. In this book only some general comments about the new methods in the AI-HOW will be made.

The Megafunction Provides "Think X"

As mentioned above, beliefs will constitute the basic units of AI-HOW manipulation. Here are some example beliefs:

1) A thing can be one or many

2) An end always follows a beginning

3) A self is not the same thing as not-self

4) A thing might exist but not appear

5) There is presently an object in front of self

6) There was an object in front of self but it has disappeared

7) A thing may come to be and then pass away

8) A command is being issued for moving an actuator

9) A command was issued yesterday for moving an actuator

Note that beliefs are already in propositional form. Beliefs can range from static beliefs drawn from metaphysics, such as distinctions like self versus other, to everyday beliefs about locations of objects.

124

Beliefs are maintained by the megafunction. While each belief can be considered independently, as a focal point of an absolute-abstraction, it is one of the main concepts of this book that nothing is really isolated and independent. It is one of the jobs of the megafunction to translate the totality of these beliefs into a single integrated changing idea. The single integrated changing absolute-abstraction changes with respect to changing beliefs and the will of the I.

Just to take a simple example drawn from our very short list of beliefs above: "a thing can be one or many" and "an end always follows a beginning." Now consider these beliefs in terms of a scenario of a sports playoff series leading to a grand champion. In the beginning we have several teams competing, and at the end only one champion. Both beliefs numbered one and two would need to come into use for this to be understood.

That is of course an extremely simple example. Now, when we say "totality" roughly what is meant by that is that all beliefs in varying degrees are taken into consideration in the creation of an understanding, which again is a single thing.

That is not to say that an understanding is simply the sum of its parts; i.e., it is not correct to say that an understanding is simply the result of the accumulation of individual beliefs. For example, I understand that today is Wednesday, but that does not mean that simply hooking together the belief that yesterday was Tuesday and tomorrow is Thursday directly results in the understanding that today is Wednesday (this is the sort of thinking which dominates contemporary computing).

For one thing, surreptitiously hidden in an understanding of days of the week are beliefs about quantity and divisibility, that is that a one week can be subdivided into subcomponents, days, which themselves are a one thing, and similar relationships apply for months and years. Also included are beliefs regarding possibility and potentiality, as for example a day that has already passed holds no more possibility, but the rest of today and the future hold possibility. But a day can't really be said to be spatial, although in a certain way each day occupies space. So when I say that I understand that today is Wednesday, that understanding is based upon a great number of beliefs such as those listed here. In fact it seems that so many beliefs are taken up in the resulting understanding that we may as well just say that *all* beliefs will be used in the AI's understanding.

It is not just that seemingly all beliefs are used to create an understanding. It is also apparent that an understanding, a concretion having a unique essence, is not the same thing as the beliefs which led to it.

Obviously we need to consider the role of reasoning. But even taking logical manipulations into consideration, the understanding which we have at any time is a singular thing, a one thing, which has a certain feel which defies formal analysis. When we understand we just understand without knowing how we understand. That has always worked for us, but in the realm of AI we are going to have to know more about the issue of understanding, and it will not be enough to just say "I understand" and leave it at that, as mostly a mystery.

A key feature, again, of this framework is that characteristics of each attribute in the matrix vary. We saw that the MIND-HOW and EXTENSION-HOW were similar in some respects but different in others. The understanding that we experience in our own minds could have certain characteristics in common with how an AI might understand – for example that beliefs together with reasoning lead to a single understanding.

Every belief will have, of course, its own potential understanding, which again the understanding includes all the other beliefs in the totality of beliefs. It is only that the focal point in the totality could change to a different belief. When the focal point changes to a given belief, the single understanding produced by the megafunction changes. And again, when a belief changes, the single understanding may change.

It could be, again, that the megafunction produces *no* understanding of a focal point given its present beliefs. More information may be needed.

Traditional raw sensor input, as mentioned above, will be one of the jobs handled by the megafunction. A great deal of research has already been done on most areas of sensor input - for example, on AI vision. A key problem here is

incorporation of sensor-derived data (possibly from
existing technology) into beliefs that are consistent with
the design of the AI-HOW.

Basically the megafunction will build most of the
absolute-abstractions – understood propositions – each
with a subjective as well as an objective component,
following roughly the Hegelian philosophy in that regard.
It is only when an inner idea of a subjective nature held
by the AI is compatible with something-is-happening in the
objective outer world that true realistic thinking and
acting can emerge in now-time.

The megafunction can build the objective side of a belief,
for example, by first establishing a focal point on some
concrete external object. The megafunction must translate
the essence of the external object into an essential
format used by the AI.

Consider a stop sign example. The megafunction would
scrutinize an image containing a stop sign. It determines
that an object in the scene is a stop sign by establishing
a focal point on a match of certain essentialities: the
object in the scene must be on the side of a road at an
intersection, must be red, must have "STOP" written on it,
and other such essentialities. It is not essential that
the sign be a very dark or light shade or red, nor is it
necessary that the sign be of a precise height, nor that
it is on a road with four lanes or two lanes. It need
only meet certain *essential* criteria to be a stop sign.

In this case the megafunction could assign a what-is-
happening noumenal-proposition of "there is a stop sign"
to a belief within an overall something-is-happening of
the totality of the outer scene. An object appears to
essentially be a stop sign having met the criteria of
possessing certain essentialities. The megafunction has
identified a particular, concrete stop sign, an objective
instance.

The question should naturally arise as to how the
megafunction knew to recognize a stop sign.

It is necessary that the megafunction be able to translate
the external format of the stop sign's essence – those
important aspects that it is displaying in a concrete form
that make it what it is – into an internal format of

essence that the AI can work with. Both humans and the AI
deal with the same *external* format of essence: a stop
sign we would expect to appear from an external, visual
perspective roughly the same for both human and AI.

It is the *internal* format of essence that will differ.
And, it is imperative that the megafunction be able to
match the external with the internal essence. Humans
somehow store essences, like that of a stop sign, in a way
which helps us to understand and recollect specific
things. We get a certain *feel* from understanding a stop
sign that is the backbone of recollection and
understanding. That feel comes from the essence. It is
not necessary that the AI have a format for internal
essence that is precisely the same as ours.

That last fact is well know, of course, to AI
practitioners, especially in the context of artificial
neural networks. A neural network, if trained to
recognize stop signs, would maintain the means of
recognition (basically the essence in more philosophical
terms) in its own format, the inner workings of which
would not readily be accessible to humans.

We can associate the completely inner component that the
AI has with the subjective, *universal* side of the
absolute-abstraction. Through repeated training or a
single adequate training instance the megafunction can
build up its stock of universals *grounded* in *particular*,
concrete instances.

For a stop sign the megafunction would ultimately retain a
belief which would contain the subjective, universal,
internal format of the essence of a stop sign that is the
result of repeated association with all of the particular,
objective cases encountered in the outer world in the
outer world's essential format. The resulting absolute-
abstraction, itself again a belief, would always
implicitly contain all of the particular cases that led to
the universal, in a fashion something like a neural
network.

In the case of a common neural network, however, generally
only those features needed to recognize an image like a
stop sign (e.g., from a video feed) have a part in
training the network. The essence of a stop sign under
this framework, however, would be built using all the
collective beliefs that are involved in creating the

understanding: that a stop sign is related to safety, is a one not a many thing, is not connected to a car directly, is usually red, has higher precedence that a yield sign, is possible to overlook, and on and on in this fashion.

It is up to the megafunction to link the inner subjective essence with the outer objective essence, and hold on to it like a dog to its bone. The entire issue of *possibility* is rooted in this relationship. The AI must be able be able to build realistic absolute-abstractions which can only be useful if the essence of the inner idea is going to conform well to the essence of the outer something-is-happening. The megafunction must determine this relationship. Without realistic possibilities the AI will be helpless in achieving its main goal.

Output in this framework has been defined as the choices made by the AI. Physical movements, learning, remembering, and even forgetting are examples of choices. When a choice is made by the self/will of the AI, its constellation of beliefs is updated accordingly by the megafunction. And again, whenever beliefs change the varying understanding can change. Thus, for example, the choice to move an actuator arm will alter the AI's belief about the location of its arm and its overall understanding of a situation.

Clearly traditional logical reasoning has a place in any form of AI. Beliefs can be gained through typical forms of logic, such as standard inference and induction procedures. From psychology, issues such as short term memory, long term memory, episodic memory and the like come into play. Each form of memory leads to a related belief.

The presentation of choices for the AI is a critical job of the megafunction. The understanding produced by the megafunction given some arbitrary focal point may result in the necessity of choosing an alternative. This is akin to the way we suddenly realize we must make a choice. Again, choice is classified as output in this framework. Choices will not be made by the megafunction, but by the oracle, as described below.

The ultimate task of the megafunction is to produce the single mega-input stream, so named because it consists of a single changing understanding of an absolute-abstraction implicitly containing the totality of beliefs, described herein, which led to it.

The mega-input stream we associate mostly with the "think X" portion of the phrase "I think X." It still remains to deal with the I.

The Oracle Provides the I

The oracle, so named in the design for Turing, has the job of making choices when provided a mega-input stream by the megafunction. The oracle can be considered as akin to a soul, the self/will as described above, and the I in the phrase "I think X." The oracle is responsible for the output of the AI.

Present forms of AI seem to be limited to "think X," meaning simply that what is thought is not held in relation to some individual I thinking. A typical chess playing program may for example have elaborate manipulations for making moves, but such moves would only be typified by such statements as "move queen to this position" and not "*I* move queen to this position," hence taking the form "think X" but not "I think X."

The lack of this fundamental relationship seemingly so common to living creatures seems to be a potentially serious oversight in AI. This framework thus makes explicit the need to represent wholly the relationship of an I which can be said to "think X."

The oracle can be thought of as atomic, a one. It is that which understands and makes rational decisions. The oracle must be able to provide grounds for its decisions, and its decisions must be good ones, which we define as those which lead to realizing the desired ends of its assignment, its main idea. The oracle is inherently motivated to fulfill its assignment as given by the human master.

Introspection is possible. The megafunction has the additional job of handling beliefs that the oracle has about itself. Thus, for example, the beliefs that the I is a one, atomic thing and that the I stands in relation to others are maintained by the oracle.

Pineal Connector Enters the Realm-of-the-What

This is the final step in the creation of AI. The so-called pineal connector, named in the design for Descartes, has the task of generating the mode-of-the-absolute, the entire "I think X" having the complete form of an absolute-abstraction as has been described herein featuring a single varying X, an understood proposition.

At this level, in the first place, the understanding output by the megafunction, based upon the totality of its beliefs, but not the same as these beliefs, *is* the singular mega-input stream to the oracle, the atomic I, and the output decisions of the oracle are input by the megafunction. Output oracle decisions update beliefs.

But in this stage we advance beyond discrete components, namely the megafunction and oracle, acting in isolation. We are now entering the realm-of-the-what, the realm of understood propositions taken together with something-is-happenings. Because the I is no longer to be separated from "think X," the connector merges all input and output into a single changing absolute-abstraction of the most basic form "I think X." Now, input and output, the I and its understanding of X cease to differentiate themselves and are one and the same thing, a single integrated totality.

The oracle is the megafunction and the megafunction is the oracle: the mega-input stream generated by the megafunction and output decisions generated by the oracle have lost their separate form and are now *united*. The I, that oracle which understands and chooses, is the choices the megafunction presents to it within the mega-input stream, each choice signaling a possible change in the focal point of the totality, a transformation of beliefs, an alteration of the understanding of a single idea, an absolute-abstraction, and the potential realization of the desired ends of its main idea assignment.

AI-TOOLBOX

Although clearly a great deal of commendable work has been done in AI already, many concepts proposed in this book are largely drawn from longstanding issues and problems in philosophy, and are not known to any present engineering science.

Conclusion

It is important to bear in mind, if nothing else, that the intent of this book has been to try to organize reality in such a fashion that AI might be shown to us, slowly revealed in a form that really already exists. We started not with a Turing machine, but by building a philosophical framework based upon reality as it can be revealed to us and only then discovering AI hidden within it. The result is a framework analogous to the way we think that can hopefully provide a starting point to work within.

It is called a framework and not a full blow system. Much work remains.

Philosophy is the best starting point for strong AI. Remember, also, that this is only an approximation – an approximation zero.

Bibliography

Works Consulted For the Philosophical Framework

Aristotle. *Categories*. Translated by E. M. Edghill.
http://classics.mit.edu/Aristotle/categories.html

Aristotle. *On Interpretation*. Translated by E. M.
Edghill.
http://classics.mit.edu/Aristotle/interpretation.html

Aristotle. *Prior Analytics*. Translated by A. J.
Jenkinson.
http://classics.mit.edu/Aristotle/prior.html

Aristotle. *Posterior Analytics*. Translated by G. R. G.
Mure.
http://classics.mit.edu/Aristotle/posterior.html

Aristotle. *Topics*. Translated by W. A. Pickard-
Cambridge.
http://classics.mit.edu/Aristotle/topics.html

Aristotle. *Metaphysics*. Translated by W. D. Ross.
http://classics.mit.edu/Aristotle/metaphysics.html

Augustine of Hippo. *Confessions*. Translated by Albert C.
Outler.
http://www.georgetown.edu/faculty/jod/augustine/conf.pdf

Berkeley, George. *A Treatise Concerning the Principles of
Human Knowledge*. http://www.gutenberg.org/ebooks/4723

Descartes, Rene. *Discourse on the Method of Rightly
Conducting One's Reason and of Seeking Truth*.
http://www.gutenberg.org/ebooks/59

Descartes, Rene. *Meditations on First Philosophy.*
Translated by Elizabeth S. Haldane.

http://www.sacred-texts.com/phi/desc/med.txt

Hegel, Georg. *Science of Logic.* Translated by A. V.
Miller. London: Allen & Unwin, 1969.

Kant, Immanuel. *The Critique of Pure Reason.* Translated
by J. M. D. Meiklejohn.
http://www.gutenberg.org/ebooks/4280

Spinoza, Baruch. *The Ethics.* Translated by R. H. M.
Elwes. Anchor Books, 1974.

Wittgenstein, Ludwig. *Tractatus Logico-Philosophicus.*
Translated by C. K. Ogden.
http://www.gutenberg.org/ebooks/5740

Selected Bibliography

1. Edited by Goertzel and Pennachin. *Artificial General Intelligence*. Springer-Verlag Berlin Heidelberg 2007. p. 132

2. Henslin, James. *Essentials of Sociology, 6th edition*. Allyn and Bacon 2006. p. 191

3. Nietzsche, Friedrich. Translated by Walter Kaufmann. "On Truth and Lie in an Extra-Moral Sense" in *The Portable Nietzsche*. Penguin Books, 1977.

4. Hume, David. *A Treatise of Human Nature*. http://www.gutenberg.org/ebooks/4705 Book II, Part III, Sec. III.

5. Aristotle. *The Ethics*. http://www.gutenberg.org/ebooks/8438 Book X.

6. Turing, Alan. "On Computable Numbers, With an Application to the Entscheidungsproblem" in *Proceedings of the London Mathematical Society*, 1936.

7. Aristotle. *Metaphysics*. Translated by W. D. Ross. http://classics.mit.edu/Aristotle/metaphysics.html Book V.

8. Searle, John. "Minds, Brains, and Programs" in the journal *The Behavioral and Brain Sciences*. 1980

9. Chalmers, David. *The Conscious Mind: In Search of a Fundamental Theory*. Oxford University Press, 1996.

10. Dennett, Daniel. *Consciousness Explained*. Back Bay Books, 1991.

11. Penrose, Roger. *Shadows of the Mind*. Oxford University Press, 1994.

12. Bunge, Mario. *Philosophical Dictionary.* Prometheus Books, 2003. p. 134 & 179.

13. Augustine of Hippo. *Confessions.* Translated by Albert C. Outler.

http://www.georgetown.edu/faculty/jod/augustine/conf.pdf Book Eleven, CHAPTER XXVIII.

14. Wittgenstein, Ludwig. *Tractatus Logico-Philosophicus.* Translated by C. K. Ogden.
http://www.gutenberg.org/ebooks/5740

15. Hegel, Georg. *Science of Logic.* Translated by A. V. Miller. London: Allen & Unwin, 1969. p. 410

16. Jones, W.T. *History of Western Philosophy.* Harcourt Brace Jovanovich, Inc. 1969. p. 189

17. Aristotle. *On the Heavens.* Translated by J. L. Stocks

http://classics.mit.edu/Aristotle/heavens.html Book I, Part 5.

18. Nietzsche, Friedrich. *Beyond Good and Evil.* Translated by R. J. Hollingdale. Penguin Books, 1973. Ch. 1

Index

Author

Mike Archbold had a lengthy career at Seafirst Bank (a subsidiary of Bank of America) in Seattle as a bank programmer. He is the author of Jazz Scale Suggester System, a jazz education "good old fashioned AI" program. In recent years he has held a variety of jobs in electronics while working on strong AI ideas. He holds a bachelor's degree in Computer Information Systems as well as an associate's degree in electronics.

www.ingramcontent.com/pod-product-compliance
Lightning Source LLC
Chambersburg PA
CBHW071002050326

40689CB00014B/3460